Science

Jean Martin Sam Ellis

Extension **7**

CAMBRIDGE
UNIVERSITY PRESS

CAMBRIDGE UNIVERSITY PRESS
Cambridge, New York, Melbourne, Madrid, Cape Town, Singapore,
São Paulo, Delhi

Cambridge University Press
The Edinburgh Building, Cambridge CB2 8RU, UK

www.cambridge.org
Information on this title: www.cambridge.org/9780521725682

First published 2008

Book printed in the United Kingdom at the University Press, Cambridge

A catalogue record for this publication is available from the British Library

ISBN 978-0-521-72568-2 paperback with CD-ROM

Contents

Introduction

Take advantage of the CD

Cambridge Essentials Science comes with a CD in the back. This contains the entire book as an interactive PDF file, which you can read on your computer using free Adobe Reader software from Adobe (www.adobe.com/products/acrobat/readstep2.html). As well as the material you can see in the book, the PDF file gives you extras when you click on the buttons you will see on most pages; see the inside front cover for a brief explanation of these.

To use the CD, simply insert it into the CD or DVD drive of your computer. You will be prompted to install the contents of the CD to your hard drive. Installing will make it easier to use the PDF file, because the installer creates an icon on your desktop that launches the PDF directly. However, it will run just as well straight from the CD.

If you want to install the contents of the disc onto your hard disc yourself, this is easily done. Just open the disc contents in your file manager (for Apple Macs, double click on the CD icon on your desktop; for Windows, open My Computer and double click on your CD drive icon), select all the files and folders and copy them wherever you want.

Take advantage of the web

Cambridge Essentials Science lets you go directly from your book to web-based activities on our website, including animations, exercises, investigations and quizzes. Access to these materials is free to all users of the book.

There are three kinds of activity, each linked to from a different place within each unit.

- **Scientific enquiry:** these buttons appear at the start and end of each unit. The activities in this section allow you to develop skills related to scientific enquiry, including experiments that would be hard to carry out in the classroom.

- **Check your progress:** these buttons come half-way through each unit. They let you check how well you have understood the unit so far.

- **Review your work:** these buttons come at the end of each unit. They let you show that you have understood the unit, or let you find areas where you need more work.

The *Teacher Material* CD-ROM for *Cambridge Essentials Science* contains enhanced interactive PDFs. As well as all the features of the pupil PDF, teachers also have links to the *Essentials Science Planner* – a new website with a full lesson planning tool, including worksheets, practicals, assessment materials, guidance and example lesson plans. The e-learning materials are also fully integrated into the Planner, letting you see the animations in context and alongside all the other materials.

7A.1 What living things are made from (HSW)

Aristotle lived in Greece over 2000 years ago. He was very interested in plants and animals, and in how the human body works. Look at the drawing by Aristotle of some parts of the human body. We call these parts **organs**.

The Greeks weren't the only people interested in how the body works. Old drawings and texts from China and the Middle East also show human organs. Some even show plant organs.

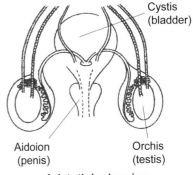

Aristotle's drawing

At first, information about organs came from surgical operations and from cutting up dead bodies. Now we can look at X-rays and body scans, too.

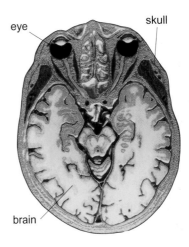

A scan through part of the head

Question 1

A closer look at human organs

In the late 18th century, a French doctor called Xavier Bichat did hundreds of post-mortems. Post-mortems are operations carried out on dead bodies to find out what killed them.

Bichat found that each human organ contains more than one kind of material. He listed 21 different kinds. Today, we call these materials **tissues**. Bichat wasn't able to see the detailed structure of these tissues because he didn't have a microscope.

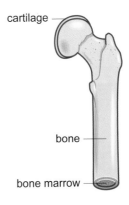

Part of a thigh bone

Question 2 **3**

7A Cells: the body's building blocks

You should already know

Outcomes

Keywords

16th century

Microscopes were invented. The lenses were not very good, so the images were not clear. The first microscopes were called <u>simple</u> microscopes. They had only one lens.

1590 Two Dutch spectacle makers, Hans and Zacharias Janssen, made a microscope with two lenses. We call this kind a <u>compound</u> microscope.

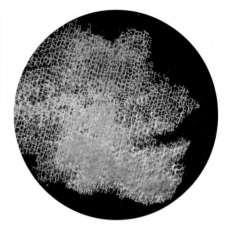

Hooke's drawing of cork cells.

17th century

English scientist Robert Hooke built a compound microscope.

1665 Hooke published the first book of drawings of microscopic structures. One of the drawings was of a slice of cork. It showed that cork is made up of what look like tiny boxes. He called these boxes **cells**.

1673 Dutchman Antonie van Leeuwenhoek found out how to make better lenses. He made a simple microscope with one of these lenses. Because his lens was better, the images were clearer than Hooke's.

1683 Leeuwenhoek published his drawings of microscopic creatures.

19th century

1831 Scotsman Robert Brown saw that there was something inside cells. He named this the **nucleus**.

1840 German scientists Matthias Schleiden and Theodor Schwann realised that all plants and animals were made of cells. They published this idea as a theory, called <u>cell theory</u>.

Leeuwenhoek's microscope.

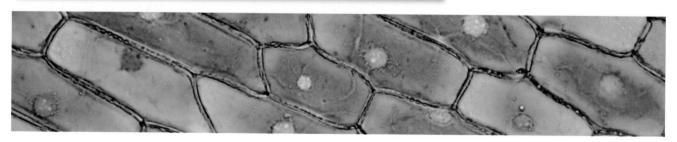

Onion cells as seen using Robert Brown's microscope.

Question 1 | 2

Scale drawings

When we draw what we see under a microscope, we draw things much bigger than they really are. We draw them to **scale**.

We often use scale drawings in our lives, not just in science.

Maps and plans are scale diagrams. They show places smaller than they really are. We call this <u>scaling down</u>.

When we show things bigger than they really are, we are <u>scaling up</u>.

You can show a scale in one of these ways:

×20   1 mm

This is the real size of a flea.

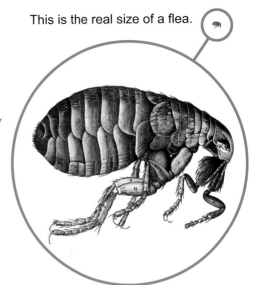

Robert Hooke drew a flea bigger than it really is. This means you can see more detail.

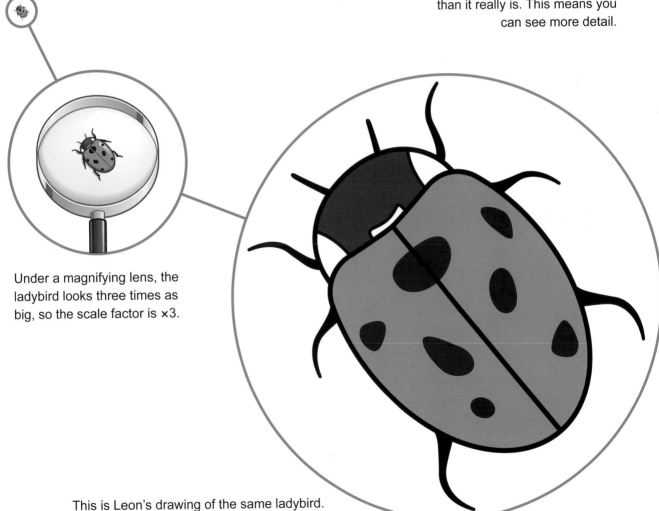

Under a magnifying lens, the ladybird looks three times as big, so the scale factor is ×3.

This is Leon's drawing of the same ladybird.

Cells are very small

Remember that all living things are made of cells and that cells are so small that you need a microscope to see them.

If you magnify cells a hundred times or more, you can see the smaller parts inside them.

Not everything has got this type of detail. Many non-living things show no structure when you look at them under a light microscope.

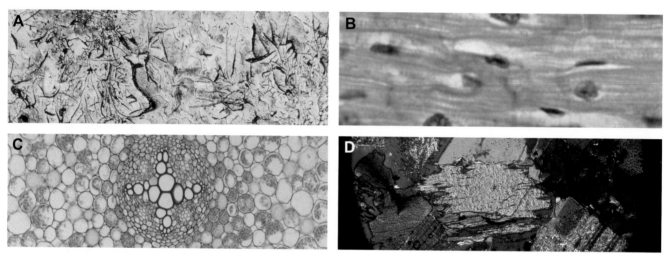

Four microscope views of living and non-living things.

Question 1

Cells are not all alike

All cells are very small. But they are not all the same size.

In this square, □, you could fit 2500 rhubarb skin cells or 10 000 human skin cells.

Cells also vary in shape.

Plant and animal cells look quite different under the microscope.

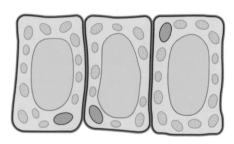

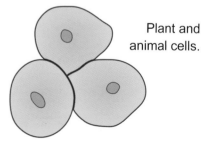

Plant and animal cells.

Question 2

A closer look at animal cells

Cells are made of lots of different parts. Each part has a different job to do to keep the cell alive and working properly.

Chris made a slide of some cheek cells.

The picture shows what they looked like under the microscope.

Chris scraped some cells from the skin inside her cheek.

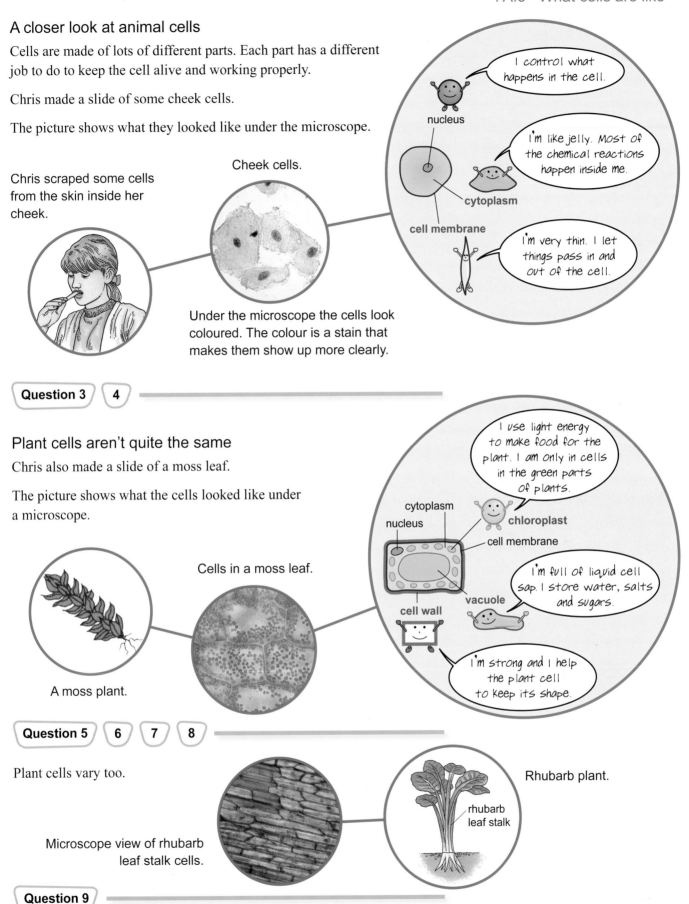

Cheek cells.

Under the microscope the cells look coloured. The colour is a stain that makes them show up more clearly.

I control what happens in the cell.

nucleus

I'm like jelly. Most of the chemical reactions happen inside me.

cytoplasm

cell membrane

I'm very thin. I let things pass in and out of the cell.

Question 3   **4**

Plant cells aren't quite the same

Chris also made a slide of a moss leaf.

The picture shows what the cells looked like under a microscope.

Cells in a moss leaf.

A moss plant.

I use light energy to make food for the plant. I am only in cells in the green parts of plants.

cytoplasm
nucleus
chloroplast
cell membrane

I'm full of liquid cell sap. I store water, salts and sugars.

vacuole
cell wall

I'm strong and I help the plant cell to keep its shape.

Question 5   **6**   **7**   **8**

Plant cells vary too.

Microscope view of rhubarb leaf stalk cells.

Rhubarb plant.

rhubarb leaf stalk

Question 9

You should already know | Outcomes | Keywords

There are over a million different types of animal. They all have different shapes and sizes. But in all these animals, there are only about 200 different kinds of cell. These cells are different because of the jobs they do, not because of the kind of animal they are found in.

Each kind of cell can do the same job in lots of different animals.

For example, when you breathe in air, you breathe in dust and micro-organisms too. They can harm your lungs. Two kinds of cells on the inside of the breathing tubes of humans and other animals help to stop this happening.

One kind makes the lining sticky with mucus. Dust and micro-organisms get trapped in this mucus. We call these cells goblet cells because of their shape. The other kind has tiny hairs that carry the mucus out of your lungs. We call these cells **ciliated epithelial cells**. (Cilia = beating hairs. Epithelium = skin or lining.)

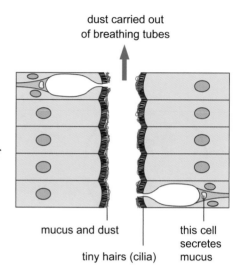

dust carried out of breathing tubes

mucus and dust | this cell secretes mucus
tiny hairs (cilia)

What the lining of your windpipe looks like.

Question 1

More specialised cells

senses in your fingers — very long nerve fibre — connections to nerve cells in your brain and spinal cord

Nerve cells are very long. They carry messages in the form of nerve impulses from one part of your body to another. Your brain and spinal cord send and receive nerve impulses from all over your body.

Red blood cells are full of a chemical called haemoglobin. This can combine with oxygen. So red blood cells can carry oxygen to every cell in the body.

It's not just animals that have special cells. Plants take water in through special cells in their roots. They are called **root hair cells**. The hairs give them a bigger surface for absorbing water.

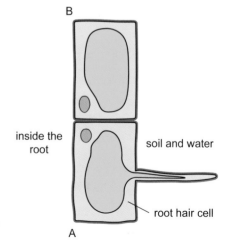

B

inside the root | soil and water

root hair cell

A

Question 2 | 3 | 4

How cells work together

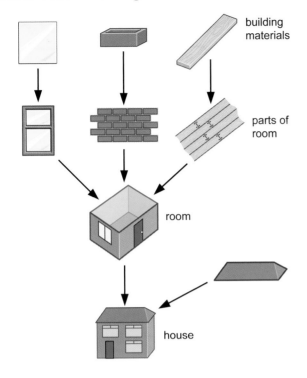

How building materials build up into a house.

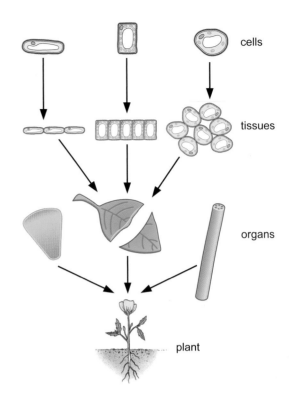

How cells build up into a plant.

A house doesn't look like a living thing. However, the way the building materials of a house are grouped is similar to the way that cells in a living thing are organised.

The bricks in a house are like the cells in a living thing. A group of bricks is called a wall. A group of similar cells is called a **tissue**. All the cells in a tissue are the same and work together to do the same job.

Question 5

In a house, different groups of building materials are joined together to make the rooms. In a living thing, several tissues are joined together to make an **organ**.

There are many different rooms in a house, and each room is needed for a different reason. In a living thing there are many different organs, and each organ has a different job.

Question 6 **7** **8**

Check your progress

You should already know

Outcomes

Keywords

People used to think that living things sometimes appeared out of nowhere. They saw for themselves that maggots appear in rotting meat. Leeuwenhoek described tiny living animals in rotting things. So the idea seemed to be sensible.

In the 19th century, Louis Pasteur proved that this idea was wrong. He showed that living things come only from other living things.

Cells are the building blocks of life. Like all living things, they don't just appear from nowhere either.

In 1858, a German scientist called Rudolph Virchow suggested that new cells could only grow from cells that were already there. Now we know that new cells form only when existing cells divide.

Question 1

How a cell divides

The nucleus divides first, then the cell. As the new cells take in more materials, they grow. When they are big enough, the cells divide again. We call this the **cell cycle**.

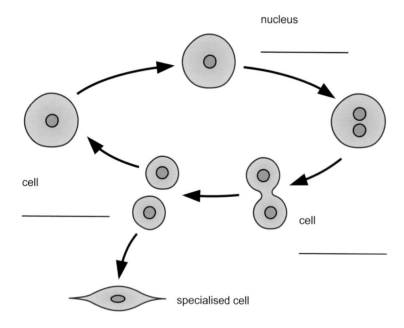

nucleus

cell

cell

specialised cell

The cell cycle.

Question 2

Plant cell division

When a plant cell divides, it's not just the nucleus and cytoplasm that divide. A new cell wall has to form between the new nuclei.

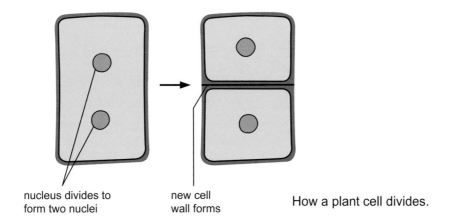

nucleus divides to form two nuclei

new cell wall forms

How a plant cell divides.

Specialised cells

Some cells divide over and over again, but other cells become specialised to do particular jobs. Specialised cells don't divide again.

Question 3 4

The nucleus controls how a cell develops

The nucleus of a cell holds all the information that tells a cell how to work and develop. Before it divides, the nucleus makes a copy of this information. One copy goes into each new nucleus. So the new cells are identical to the old ones.

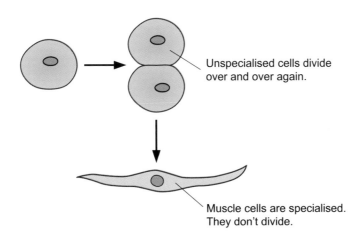

Unspecialised cells divide over and over again.

Muscle cells are specialised. They don't divide.

Review your work

Question 5

Summary ➡

You should already know   Outcomes   Keywords

New evidence, new explanations

Just like detectives, scientists try to explain the **evidence** that they collect.

They suggest **theories** based on the evidence they have at the time.

With new evidence, they may change their ideas and suggest new theories.

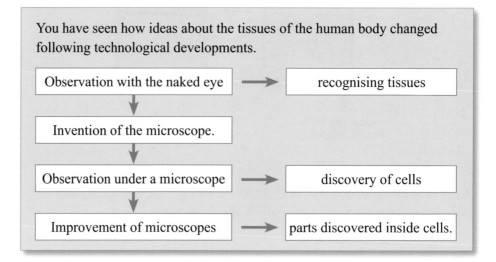

You have seen how ideas about the tissues of the human body changed following technological developments.

Observation with the naked eye → recognising tissues

Invention of the microscope.

Observation under a microscope → discovery of cells

Improvement of microscopes → parts discovered inside cells.

Question 1

During the 17th and early 18th centuries, people improved both lenses and microscopes. Only after German instrument manufacturer Carl Zeiss teamed up with Ernst Abbe in 1866 did the next big change take place. Zeiss asked Abbe to use <u>optics theory</u> to design a better microscope.

Abbe's first systems didn't work so he began to do <u>experiments</u>, not just with lenses but on what happens to light as it passes through lenses to form an image. From a series of experiments, he was able:

- to suggest a theory about how microscope images formed;
- to test his theory by doing more experiments;
- then to put his theory into practice in his designs.

Studying cells is part of <u>biology</u>

Studying light and optics is part of <u>physics</u>.

Applying science is <u>technology</u>.

The story of cells shows the importance of working together.

Question 2 **3**

One theory that came out of Abbe's experiments was a limit to what can be seen clearly using a light microscope. He predicted that future 'microscopes' might not limited by the properties of light. That prediction came true with the invention of electron microscopes. These use a beam of electrons rather than light.

Scientists gather evidence by **observing** and **experimenting**.

They use the evidence to make theories – and then gather more evidence to test those theories.

Question 4

Changing ideas about babies

Ideas about where babies come from also changed with the invention of the microscope.

If you had lived more than 250 years ago, you probably didn't know exactly where babies came from. Look at the table.

> New evidence changed ideas about reproduction.

Evidence	Who and when	Fluid passed from a man into a woman to make a baby contains …
A fluid (semen) was involved.	Hippocrates (about 2500 years ago)	… tiny body parts.
Under a microscope, they could see tiny swimming things in semen.	Antonie van Leeuwenhoek, Nicolas Hartsoeker, others (over 300 years ago)	… 'animalcules'. Some scientists claimed to see miniature humans inside the animalcules from humans. They were called <u>homunculi</u>, the Latin world for 'little men'.
Experiments showed that both sperm and egg cell were needed to make a baby.	Lazzaro Spallanzani (about 200 years ago)	… sperm that joined with a woman's egg cell.

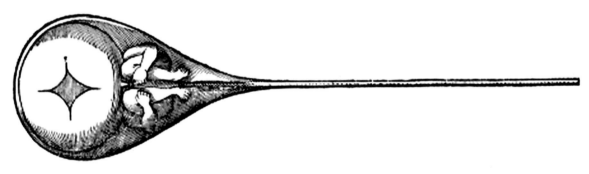

A homunculus in a sperm.
(The plural is homunculi.)

(Question 5) (6) ──────────

You should already know | Outcomes | Keywords

All plants and animals die. So some of each kind must produce young so that their kind survives. This is **reproduction**.

In many plants and animals, a new life starts when the nuclei of two sex cells join. One of these sex cells comes from the male, the other from the female. We call this kind of reproduction <u>sexual reproduction</u>.

Sex cells and fertilisation in plants

Flowers are the reproductive systems of plants. Their job is to make seeds that can grow into new plants. Flowers produce special sex cells. Pollen contains the male sex cell and the ovule contains the female sex cell.

Pollen has to travel from the male part of a plant to the female part of the same plant or of another plant of the same species. This is **pollination**.

Pollen travels from the anther to the stigma of a flower of the same species. This is called pollination.

Question 1 / 2 / 3

Then the pollen grows a tube down to the ovule. The nucleus of the male sex cell travels down this tube to join with the nucleus of the ovule.

We call the joining of the male and female sex cells **fertilisation**.

The cell that forms in fertilisation is the first cell of the new plant.

This cell then grows and divides to make a seed.

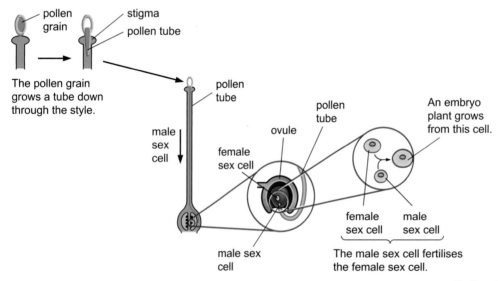

Pollen-tube growth and fertilisation.

Question 4 / 5

Comparing fertilisation in plants and animals

In plants

A pollen grain has a tough outer wall. A tube grows

- out of the grain
- into the stigma
- through the style
- to the ovary.

The male sex cell travels down this tube to reach the ovule.

pollen grain

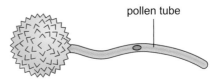

pollen tube

Pollen grain growing
a pollen tube.

Question 6

In animals

The male sex cell is always inside the body or in water so it doesn't dry up.

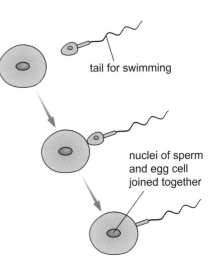

tail for swimming

nuclei of sperm
and egg cell
joined together

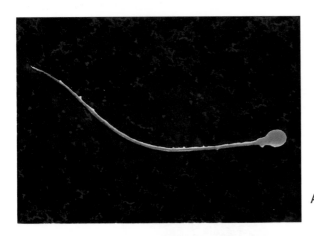

A male sex cell.
We call it a sperm.
A sperm swims to reach
an egg.

A new life starts when the
nucleus of a sperm joins with
the nucleus of an egg cell.
We say that the nuclei fuse.
This fusing is called fertilisation.

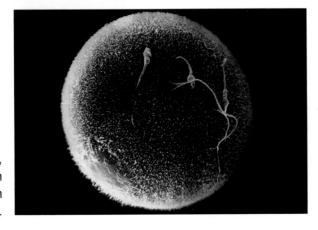

This female sex cell,
or egg cell, is much
bigger than the sperm
cells around it.

 Question 7 **8**

Patterns of reproduction in animals

Different animals fertilise their eggs in different ways. Male fish and male frogs fertilise the egg cells outside the female's body. We call this <u>external fertilisation</u>. The egg cells of birds and mammals are fertilised inside the female's body. We call this <u>internal fertilisation</u>.

Look at the pictures. The eggs of fish and frogs don't have shells. They would dry up if they were laid on land, so they are laid in water. Each egg contains only a little stored food.

Most frogs and fish don't look after their eggs and young. They need to lay lots of eggs to make sure that a few survive.

Penguins are birds. They lay one or two eggs. Each egg contains lots of stored food.

Mammals are different again. Their young grow in a special organ inside the mother's body. We call this organ the uterus. After they are born, one or both parents feed and protect their young until they can look after themselves.

Penguins look after their eggs and young.

Cats look after their young until they are old enough to find their own food and protect themselves.

Question 9 10 11 12 13

7B.2 Reproduction and development of humans

You should already know	Outcomes	Keywords

Humans are mammals. So:

- human eggs have no shell;
- fertilisation happens inside the mother's body;
- the young develop in the mother's uterus;
- after they are born, the young feed on milk;
- one or both parents look after the young.

Often, other adults and older children help too.

Question 1

A woman releases an egg cell from one of her ovaries about once a month. This is called **ovulation**. Fertilisation can happen only as the egg cell travels down an oviduct. When sperm cells meet an egg cell, the sperm make a special chemical to break down the outer part of the egg cell. Then the nucleus of one sperm can join with the nucleus of the egg cell. We say that the egg cell is fertilised when this happens.

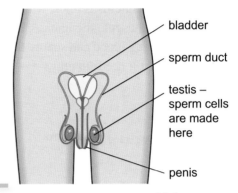

Male organs.

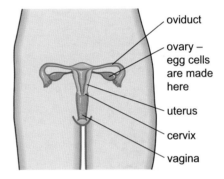

Female organs.

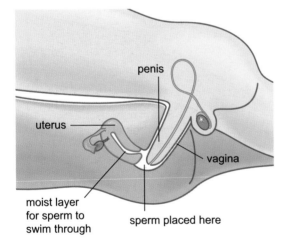

Over 200 million sperm cells travel from the testes through the penis and into the vagina.

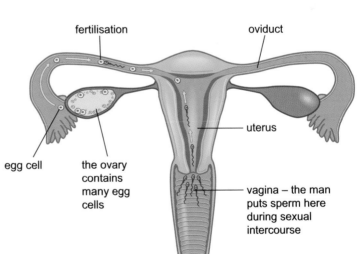

The sperm and egg cells are really much smaller than this diagram shows. An egg cell is the size of a tiny speck of sand. You need a microscope to see sperm.

Question 2 **3** **4**

From fertilised egg to baby

Once the egg cell has been fertilised, it grows and divides as it travels down the oviduct into the uterus. First it forms two cells, then four cells, then eight cells. By the time it reaches the uterus, it is a whole ball of cells called an **embryo**.

The lining of the uterus is thick, with lots of blood vessels. The embryo settles into the lining. This is called **implantation**. Now the mother's blood can supply the embryo with the food and oxygen that it needs to grow.

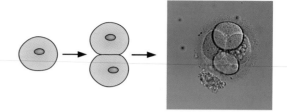

Cells split over and over again.

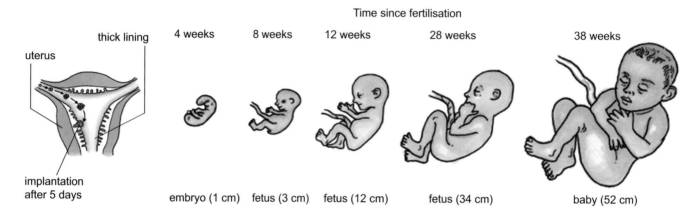

Time since fertilisation

thick lining | 4 weeks | 8 weeks | 12 weeks | 28 weeks | 38 weeks

uterus

implantation after 5 days

embryo (1 cm)   fetus (3 cm)   fetus (12 cm)   fetus (34 cm)   baby (52 cm)

Growth of the embryo, fetus and baby after implantation. (The pictures are not to scale.)

Question 5 6 7

Why children are like their parents

The nuclei of sex cells contain the information for making a new life. So the fertilised egg cell **inherits** from each parent some of the information that determines the features of the baby.

That is why parents, a child and its brothers and sisters have some features in common.

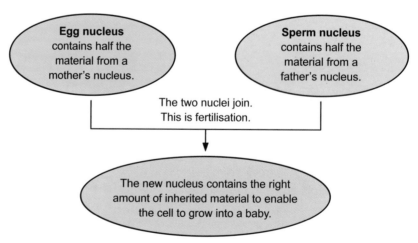

Egg nucleus contains half the material from a mother's nucleus.

Sperm nucleus contains half the material from a father's nucleus.

The two nuclei join. This is fertilisation.

The new nucleus contains the right amount of inherited material to enable the cell to grow into a baby.

Half of the inherited material came from the mother and half from the father. So the baby will have some features from each parent.

Question 8

Some brothers and sisters are more alike than others

Twins are born at the same time. They can be identical or non-identical.

The twins in the first picture grew after two egg cells were fertilised by two different sperm. They inherited some of the same features from their parents, but they also inherited some features that are not the same. So, they are non-identical twins.

The twins in the second picture grew after one fertilised egg cell divided to form two separate embryos. They inherited the same pattern from their parents, so they are identical twins.

Non-identical twins.

Identical twins.

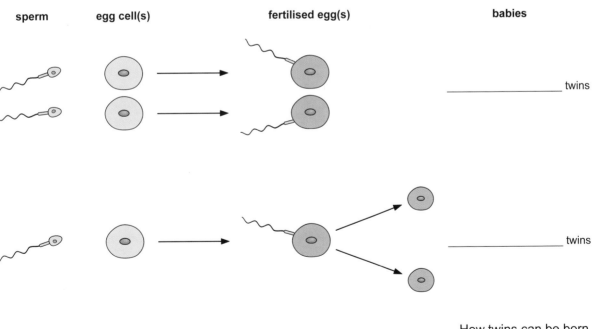

How twins can be born.

Question 9   10

You should already know

Outcomes

Keywords

To survive and grow, an embryo has to be implanted in the lining of the uterus. For this to happen, the uterus lining must be ready for it.

Timing is important. There is a cycle that links the release of an ovum (egg cell) to the development of the uterus lining. This cycle is called the **menstrual cycle**. Each menstrual cycle lasts about a month.

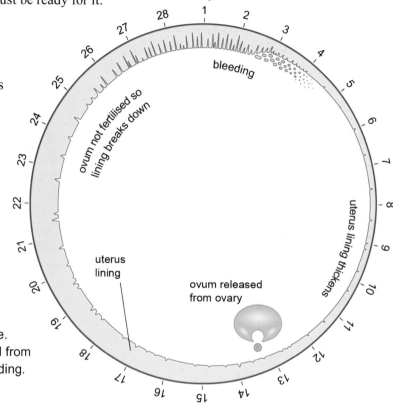

The menstrual cycle.
Days are numbered from
the first day of bleeding.

Question 1   2

Special chemicals called **hormones** control the menstrual cycle. These chemicals are so powerful that they can even change how a woman feels at different times in the cycle.

If an egg is not fertilised, the lining of the uterus breaks down.

The woman 'bleeds', or has a 'period'. We call this bleeding **menstruation**. If an egg is fertilised and an embryo is implanted, the lining does not break down. Menstruation stops.

Question 3   4   5

7B.4 The uterus as home to the developing baby

You should already know | Outcomes | Keywords

The mother's body keeps the **fetus** at a constant temperature.

The thick muscular wall of the uterus stretches as the fetus grows.

A special organ called the **placenta** grows in the lining. Substances can pass across the placenta between the blood of the fetus and the blood of the mother. But the blood of fetus and mother do not mix.

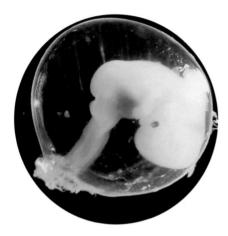

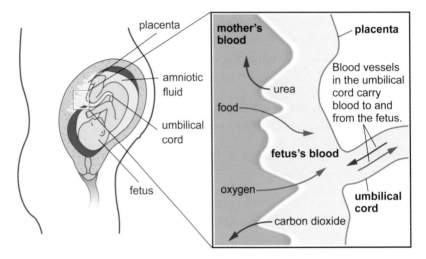

There is a bag of thin skin around the embryo. This bag is full of a liquid called **amniotic fluid**. This fluid supports the embryo and protects it against shocks.

As the embryo grows, it becomes a fetus. The placenta supplies the fetus with food and oxygen and takes away waste materials.

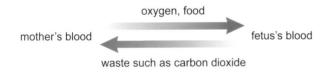

Question 1 | 2

Sadly, harmful substances, such as alcohol and other drugs, can also pass into the fetus's blood. Some of them can harm the fetus as it grows.

- On average, babies born to mothers who smoke weigh less and have more health problems than babies born to non-smokers.
- A few babies are born addicted to alcohol or other drugs.
- Rubella (German measles) is a virus infection. If a mother gets it in the first three months of pregnancy, her baby may be born deaf and blind.

Question 3 | Check your progress

[You should already know] [Outcomes] [Keywords]

Childbirth

We call childbirth 'labour' because it is hard work. When a baby is born, it passes out of the uterus and through the vagina into the outside world.

Before this can happen, a strong muscle around the opening of the uterus must relax and open up. This muscle is part of the cervix.

When the baby is ready to be born, many strong contractions of the muscles of the uterus pull the cervix open. Once the cervix is open, the baby's head can go down into the vagina. Then the mother has to use the muscles of her abdomen, too. She has to push hard to get the baby out.

The next job is to make sure that there is no fluid in the baby's nose and mouth, so that it can take its first breath.

A short time later, contractions of the uterus push the placenta out, too. We call this the afterbirth.

The newborn baby is cleaned, checked to make sure that there are no problems and then wrapped up to keep it warm.

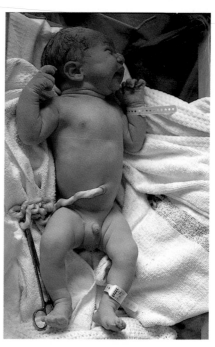

The **umbilical cord** is clamped before it is cut.

[Question 1] [2] [3]

Baby care

Looking after a baby is also hard work. Human babies are entirely dependent on their parents and other adults.

Babies need protection against disease, accidents and animals.

Babies need to be kept clean.

The natural food for young mammals is milk from the **mammary glands**. The composition of milk is different in different mammals. Many human mothers prefer to feed their babies using their own breast milk. This milk contains substances that destroy some of the micro-organisms that cause infections in humans. So it also helps to protect the baby against these infections.

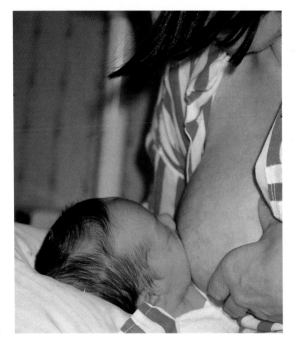

Babies need food and warmth.

Question 4

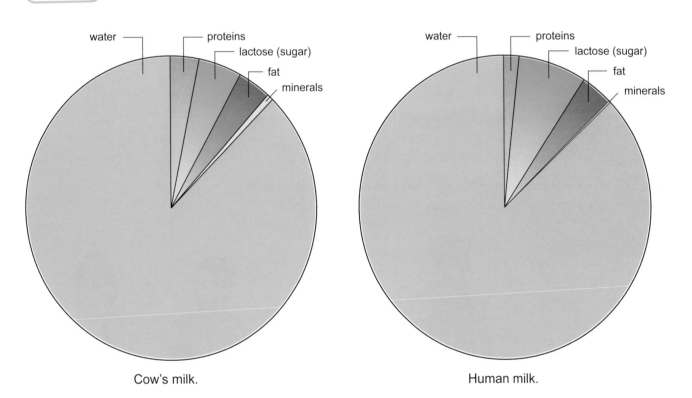

Cow's milk.

Human milk.

Human children depend on adults for many years. Babies have to learn to control their bodies, to talk and to walk. Usually many adults and older children help to care for them and to teach them. Children also learn many things for themselves.

Question 5 **6** **7**

| You should already know | Outcomes | Keywords |

Some children grow up faster than others. But all children grow faster at certain times. Children also change as they grow.

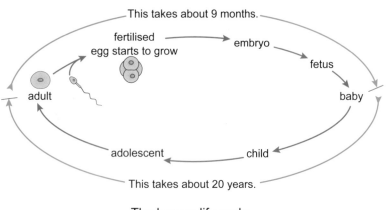

The human life cycle.

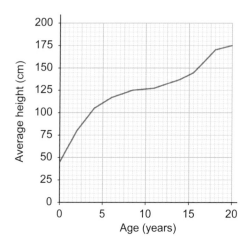

Growth between birth and 20 years of age.

Question 1

Sometimes it is difficult to tell whether a young child is a boy or a girl.

Before birth and in the early years, a child's head grows faster than its body. Later, the body grows faster, and boys and girls start to look less alike.

Children grow quickly from babies to toddlers.

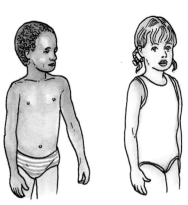

Young boys and girls have the same body shape.

Question 2

A time of rapid growth and change starts in the early teens, at anything between 9 and 16 years old. Often the changes start earlier in girls than in boys. We call the time between childhood and adulthood **adolescence**.

At this time, a gland in the brain starts to make extra **hormones**. These are special chemicals that make cells grow and divide faster. They also make the testes and ovaries mature and produce sex hormones. At **puberty**, the mature testes and ovaries start to release sex cells.

 Question 3

The testes and ovaries make different hormones. So boys and girls develop in different ways.

Body parts other than the sex organs develop special features. We call these features **secondary sexual characteristics**. When these develop, it becomes easier to tell a boy from a girl.

Girls	Boys
pubic and underarm hair grows	pubic and underarm hair grows
breasts grow	facial and body hair grows
ovaries start to release eggs	voice deepens
monthly periods (of bleeding) begin	testes start to make sperm

 Question 4   5

Sex hormones also cause emotional changes and affect behaviour.

So adolescence is often a difficult time, especially because changes take place at different rates in different young people.

Question 6

Women develop broader hips and breasts as they grow up.

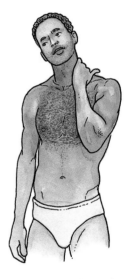

Usually, men have broader chests and shoulders and more muscle than women.

Review your work

Summary ➡

You should already know | Outcomes | Keywords

Having a baby is sometimes a problem

So far, we have looked only at how humans make embryos and how babies then develop. But some couples need the help of doctors and technology to make a baby.

There are several possible reasons for this.

- The woman doesn't release egg cells.
- The man doesn't make sperm or makes faulty sperm.
- The woman's egg tubes are blocked. This can happen as a result of having an untreated **sexually transmitted disease**.
- There is a risk of a baby inheriting a genetic disorder.

Information

Sexually transmitted diseases pass from one person to another when they have sex. Using condoms can prevent transfer of the bacteria and viruses that cause these diseases. Early treatment is important.

Question 1 **2**

Helping people to reproduce

Doctors start by investigating whether the couple is producing sperm and egg cells, and whether the woman's egg tubes are blocked.

If so they can try **IVF** (*in vitro* **fertilisation**). They may use

- the couple's own egg cells and sperm
- sperm or egg cells from donors.

They implant the fertilised embryos in the uterus (womb), but the embryos don't always grow.

In IVF, egg cells are fertilised in a dish and then placed in the woman's womb.

Question 3 **4** **5**

Doctors collected lots of data on the success rates of IVF. They used to implant three or four embryos. But, for some women, this didn't make a pregnancy more likely. Other women produced triplets or quads. These are more likely to be born too early and to die.

Now the authorities suggest implanting two embryos at the most.

This decision was based on evidence.

Question 6

We can do it – but should we?

Scientists developed reproductive technologies by applying what they knew about reproduction. IVF is one of those technologies. It has improved some people's lives.

But some people think that it shouldn't be allowed. With any developments in science and technology, we have to ask what we do with them. We need to think about:

- whether or not we use them;
- how we use them.

We shouldn't interfere with nature.

I'd rather the money was spent on treating heart disease and cancer.

We could be producing children who'll need IVF themselves.

I'd never have had my baby without IVF.

It's against my religion.

When you make decisions about issues such as the use of IVF, you are thinking about **ethics**. To make a decision, you need:

- to understand what can be done;
- to think of the advantages and disadvantages of each alternative;
- to decide what you think and to give your reasons.

These decisions are based on ethics and evidence.

Question 7 8

Some ways of investigating

There are different ways of doing investigations. So the first thing to do is to decide which way will give you the answers to your question.

- You could do a laboratory investigation – make your own observations and do your own experiments.
- You could use secondary sources. Information collected by other people to help you to answer a question is called **secondary data**.
- You could do field work. You can observe the behaviour of animals or use sampling to do **surveys** of a habitat or of people. Questionnaires are useful for collecting data or opinions from people.

> You have to use secondary sources to find out about the behaviour of large animals.

Question 1 / 2

Investigations using living things

When you plan an investigation such as the one about the behaviour of woodlice on page 31, you need to think about:

- safety;
- the equipment you will use and how you will use it;
- how to make your test fair.

Sometimes you need to use apparatus, chemicals or living things that can be harmful. We call these things **hazards**. You can use them only if you make sure that you and other people are safe. You can look up some hazards in books, or you can ask your teacher for help.

Next you need to ask yourself how high a **risk** there is of the hazard causing harm. We call this a **risk assessment**. You do this to find out if your investigation is safe to do. Sometimes the risk assessment helps you to see how to make it safe, for example by wearing eye protection.

Question 3

Enzymes in washing powder make my skin red and sore.

Locusts give me a rash.

Peanuts make me very ill.

When you investigate living things, you need to avoid animals, plants and enzymes that you are allergic to.

Fair testing in an animal behaviour investigation

In an experiment, lots of things affect the results. We call these **variables**. We need to

- vary the thing we are trying to find out about;
- control the other variables (this means keeping them the same).

Variables such as light and temperature are fairly easy to control. It is harder to deal with the variation in living things. So you need to gather data about a large **sample** of living things to allow for their variability.

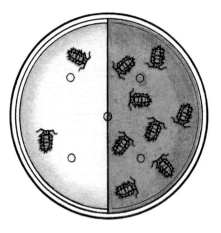

Woodlice vary. They might not all behave in the same way. So there are ten in this experiment and the experiment is repeated five times.

Question 4

Investigating by observing

Some scientists find out about animal behaviour by watching them in the wild.

For example, Karl von Frisch watched bees and their hives. He discovered that they were able to 'tell' each other where to collect nectar to make honey. He learned the movements that they made to pass on information about both the direction and the distance to the food.

He called these movements the 'waggle dance'.

Question 5

Investigating animal behaviour using secondary sources

If you can't do your own investigations, you can use libraries and the Internet. You need to make sure that you can use:

- library catalogues;
- the index and contents page of a book;
- a search engine on the Internet.

The bee in the middle is dancing to tell the other bees where to find pollen. The dancing bee has just returned from a successful trip to find food. You can just see the full pollen sacs on its legs.

Question 6

In the rest of this Unit, you will find examples of how living things and their habitats are studied by observing and measuring in both fieldwork and laboratory work.

7C.1 Habitats

| You should already know | Outcomes | Keywords |

Habitats are places where plants and animals live. Your body is a habitat. Your skin is home to as many micro-organisms as there are people on Earth! Sometimes fleas, lice, flatworms and roundworms make their homes in or on your body.

A pond is a habitat with:

- fresh (not salty) water;
- a small temperature range;
- less light as you go deeper;
- less oxygen as you go deeper;
- a range of food sources.

A plant or animal's habitat provides the right conditions for it to survive. Each plant or animal has features that suit it to the conditions. We say that the plant or animal is **adapted** to these **environmental conditions**.

rock to hibernate under

It is damp and shady under plants.

eggs

newt tadpoles

insects and other small animals to eat

A pond is a watery habitat.

Look at the pictures of the newt tadpoles and the newt. The tadpoles are smaller than the adult newt, with no legs and with gills instead of lungs. They spend all their time in the water.

muscular tail for swimming

mottled skin for camouflage

Oxygen goes in through the newt's lungs and damp skin.

legs for walking and swimming

A great crested newt.

Question 1

Plants need light to make food, so their leaves need to be near or above the surface of the water.

Environmental conditions, such as the amount of light or water, are different in different habitats. So different habitats support different plants and animals.

Two land habitats.

Grassland	Woodland
plenty of light	trees shade the ground
fairly large range of temperatures	smaller range of temperatures
exposed to the wind	sheltered from the wind
fairly dry soil	damper soil
less humid air	more humid air

some animals shelter among plants, whereas others burrow in the soil	animals live in trees and other plants, in leaf litter and in burrows

Adaptations

Some adaptations for burrowing are:

- a cylindrical or streamlined shape;
- strong legs and clawed feet;
- good senses of
  - smell
  - vibration.

(Burrowers often have a poor sense of sight.)

A mole has strong claws for digging.

An earthworm has a long thin body and slimy skin.

A song thrush.

Question 2 3 4

You should already know	Outcomes	Keywords

Conditions such as light and temperature are different in different habitats. These conditions also vary over a 24-hour period.

Marcus wanted to measure changes in temperature in the school greenhouse. He used a datalogger and a thermometer so that he could compare the results. (A datalogger collects and records information.)

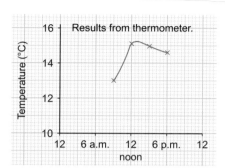

Question 1 / **2**

The charts show Marcus's results. He can record daily changes in the amounts of light, sound and water vapour in similar ways.

Like you, other animals and plants are adapted to daily changes.

Some animals are up and about during the day, some at night. Bats and owls are adapted to feed at night. We call them **nocturnal** animals. Other animals are active when it is getting light or getting dark. So you see different animals at different times.

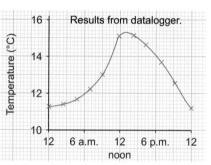

Before school	During school	After school	Getting dark	After dark
squirrels	butterflies	butterflies	sparrows	bats
sparrows	bees	bees	midges	foxes
blackbirds	sparrows	squirrels	bats	owls
rabbits	kestrels	sparrows	foxes	moths
		kestrels	mice	earthworms

Animals seen or heard in a school garden at different times of the day.

Question 3 / **4** / **5**

Bats send out sounds and listen for echoes using their sensitive ears. Bats that feed on flying insects have small eyes. Bats that feed on nectar have large eyes.

Livingstone daises open only in the sunshine.

This bat feeds on the nectar of banana flowers, which are open at night.

Owls hear well and can see in dim light.

Investigating behaviour

Science isn't just about what other people have found out. It is also about finding things out for yourself. You can ask questions. Then you can do **investigations** to find out the answers.

Question 6

For example, you might:

- want to find out about the behaviour of woodlice;
- suggest reasons why woodlice hide under stones;
- test one of your ideas using a choice chamber.

The woodlouse in the picture has a choice between dark and light.

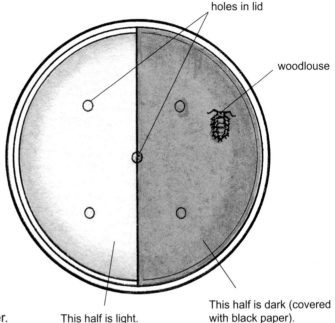

holes in lid

woodlouse

A woodlouse in a choice chamber.

This half is light.

This half is dark (covered with black paper).

Question 7

You may say what you think will happen. We call that making a **prediction**. Scientists often make predictions. Then they test their predictions to see whether they are right.

Even if the woodlouse stopped in the side that you predicted for a long time, you couldn't be sure that your prediction was correct for all woodlice. There are many different kinds of woodlouse, and within each kind the woodlice vary. You need to think about variation when you investigate an animal for yourself.

You will also need to think about which environmental conditions you will vary and which you will keep the same.

Question 8   9

Woodlice are born with this behaviour. We say it is **instinctive**.

Some behaviour is learned. Scientists do experiments to study that.

Other scientists are interested in social behaviour – how animals interact in families and other groups. They **observe** this behaviour.

Three different kinds of woodlouse.

Seasonal change

Environmental conditions change with the **seasons**. Plants and animals must be adapted to these changes to survive. In the UK, the cold and frost of winter are problems for many plants and animals. We call these difficult conditions **climatic stresses**.

Climatic stresses vary from place to place. In some places the problem is shortage of water; in others it is high temperatures.

spring

winter   summer

autumn

The seasons of the year.

There are fewer hours of daylight in winter.

Question 10

Plants lose a lot of water from their leaves. When it is cold they cannot take any more water in. Also, winter frosts damage some leaves. So many plants get rid of their leaves before the frosts start. We call trees that lose their leaves at a particular time of year deciduous trees. Evergreen trees keep their leaves all the year round.

Question 11   **12**

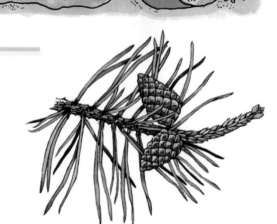

Pine needles are tough so that they can withstand the cold. Their small surface area and waxy surface help to reduce water loss.

Plants that lose their leaves can't make food in winter. We say that they are dormant. They use their stores of food to grow new leaves in spring.

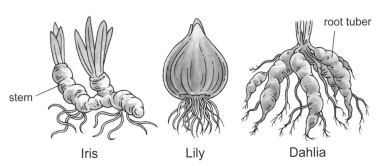

stem

Iris   Lily   Dahlia

Some plants live through the winter as roots, stems or bulbs under the ground. All the parts above the ground die.

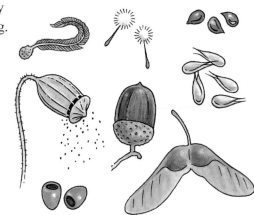

root tuber

Plants can also survive the winter as seeds.

Question 13   14   15

Seasonal behaviour patterns in animals

The British winter brings problems for animals, too. It's cold and there isn't much food, because there are fewer leaves and insects about. Most of the insects that we see in summer live through winter as eggs or pupae. Both of these are hidden away.

Some birds fly south to warmer climates for winter. We say that they **migrate**. Other animals go into a deep sleep – they **hibernate**. Their hearts slow down and their temperatures drop. Their bodies slow right down so that stored fat is used up very slowly through winter.

Some butterflies hibernate. Many survive the winter as pupae. Adults come out of the pupae in spring.

When it is winter in the UK, it is warmer in Africa and there are insects for swallows to eat.

During hibernation, hedgehogs use fat stored in their bodies.

Question 16

Other animals stay active all the year round. In autumn, these birds and mammals store extra fat and grow a thicker coat of fur or feathers for insulation. Some change colour for better **camouflage**.

Rabbits get fatter and grow a thicker coat to prepare for winter.

Question 17   18

Check your progress

Plants make their own food. Plants are called **producers** because they produce the food. Animals feed on plants or on animals that have eaten plants so we call them **consumers**. Animals that are adapted to eating plants are called **herbivores**. Other animals are adapted to eating animal flesh. They are **carnivores**. Some carnivores hunt and kill living animals. These are **predators**. The animals that they hunt are their **prey**. Prey animals are adapted to escape or to hide from predators.

Predators	Prey
owl	snail
fox	vole
shark	antelope
leopard	fly
spider	rabbit
eel	plaice
mantis	greenfly

Question 1 2 3   4

Food chains

A **food chain** shows what eats what.

Food chains begin with green plants because only green plants make food. The arrows show the direction of **energy transfer** along the food chain.

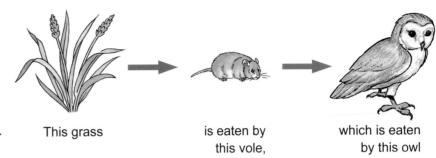

This grass

is eaten by this vole,

which is eaten by this owl

 Question 5 **6**

The arrows also show the way that energy is transferred along food chains. When they make food, green plants take energy from sunlight. When an animal eats a plant, the energy is transferred to the animal.

Question 7

Food webs

Voles don't feed on grass alone, and owls don't just eat voles. Plants and animals usually belong to more than one food chain. So, we join food chains to make a **food web** for a habitat.

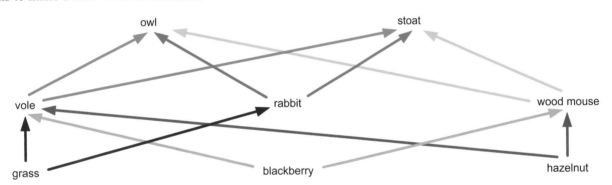

Part of a food web for a hedgerow.

 Question 8 **9**

Green plants transfer energy from sunlight into the web as food. So if all the plants disappear, there is no food for the animals in the habitat.

A change in the number of animals also affects food webs. For example, if all the owls die:

- the population of animals that the owls usually eat goes up;
- there will be more food for stoats so the number of stoats goes up;
- rabbits, voles and mice **compete** for food. If there are too many of them, some won't get enough to eat. Some will die and their numbers will go down.

Review your work

Summary ➡

Question 10

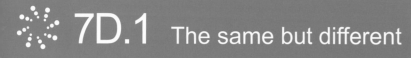

7D.1 The same but different

You should already know | Outcomes | Keywords

A **species** is one kind of living thing. Members of a species:

- are very much alike (we say that a lot of their **characteristics** are the same);
- are different from members of other species;
- produce fertile offspring only when they breed with each other.

Humans are all similar. They can reproduce and produce fertile offspring. So we say that they belong to the same species.

Humans all belong to the same species.

Question 1 2

Variety is the spice of life!

Even though humans share many characteristics, there are differences between them. We say that they **vary**. We call the differences **variations**. Some of the differences are easy to see. Other differences are difficult or impossible to see.

All these girls have different blood groups.

Question 3 4

Variations in other animals and plants

We have seen how humans vary. Other animals vary too. Dogs look different because they are different breeds. But they are all members of the same species.

A family tree for a basset hound, a terrier, a labrador and their offspring.

Question 5 **6**

Plants from the same species also vary. Corn is one species of plant. Its fruits are called cobs. We use different varieties for sweetcorn, animal food, popcorn, cornflour and cornflakes.

Corncobs come in different shapes, sizes and colours. We call these <u>varieties</u> of corn.

Question 7 **8**

Variations in a characteristic often run in families. They pass from one generation to the next. We call them **inherited variations**. But not all variations are inherited.

Some characteristics vary because of the environment in which a living thing develops. Other variations have a mixture of inherited and environmental causes.

Variations that run in families

The Habsburg family was one of the ruling families of Europe. Many members had a lip characteristic of the family. It is called the Habsburg lip.

Emperor Maximillian (1459–1519).

Maximillian's grandson, Emperor Charles V (1500–1558).

Archduke Charles of Teschen (1771–1847).

Question 1 / 2

How we find patterns of inheritance

We can use a diagram to show how people are related to each other.

We call this diagram a **family tree**. A family tree can also show how a characteristic is inherited. We can see if a characteristic passes from parents to children. A characteristic is inherited when we see a strong pattern in a family tree.

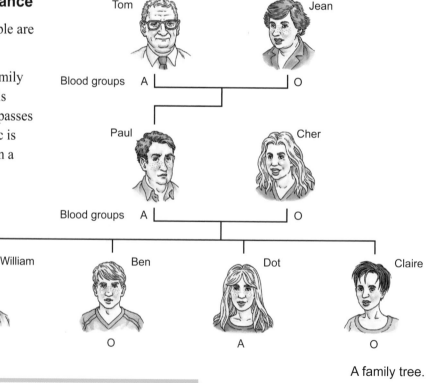

Tom   Jean

Blood groups   A   O

Paul   Cher

Blood groups   A   O

William   Ben   Dot   Claire

Blood groups   A   O   A   O

A family tree.

Question 3 / 4 / 5 / 6

Environmental variations

Environmental variations are not inherited. They develop as a result of what happens to an animal or plant during its lifetime.

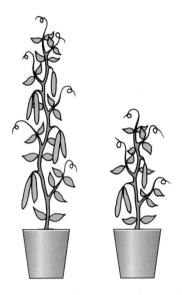

These pea plants grew in exactly the same environmental conditions.

This is how leeks grow. These leeks are all the same variety.

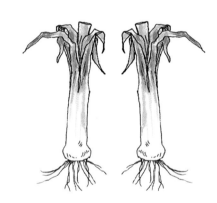

Leeks from the centre of the garden.

Question 7 8

Joan and Ellen are identical twins. Ellen had a serious illness when she was nine, so she did not grow as tall as her sister.

Leeks from the edge of the garden.

Question 9 10

You should already know | Outcomes | Keywords

We have seen that there can be lots of variation between members of the same species. But there is more variation between members of different species.

Gorillas are similar to humans in some ways. But they also have characteristics that are different from those of humans. So gorillas belong to a different species.

Gorilla.

Question 1

When you look for differences between a human and a gorilla, you have to look carefully. Careful observation is very important in science.

Books for identifying plants and animals use drawings and detailed descriptions to help us to tell one species from another. Descriptions in stories and poems don't have to be so accurate. They are sometimes about only one characteristic.

Who is this...

Question 2

...in the poem?

> There once was a _____ called Nick
> whose movements were sudden and quick.
> He loved to pop out
> and cause people to shout
> but his wriggling legs made me sick!

Question 3

...in the scientific description?

> Nick has eight legs.
> He has two parts to his body, a head and an abdomen.
> He has spinnerets that he uses to make silken threads.
> He has hard outer parts called an exoskeleton to protect him.
> Nick eats insects, so he is a carnivore.

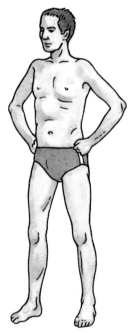

Human.

Question 4 5 6 7

Why details are important

Hoverflies and wasps look similar in many ways. However, wasps sting and hoverflies don't. Many people like to see hoverflies in their gardens because hoverfly young eat the greenfly that damage their plants.

Scientific description of hoverflies	Scientific description of common wasps
have a head, a thorax and an abdomen	have a head, a thorax and an abdomen
have six jointed legs	have six jointed legs
have bright black-and-yellow markings on their abdomen	have bright black-and-yellow markings on their abdomen
often feed on pollen and nectar from flowers	like sugary foods but mainly feed on meat
can hover	do not hover
have a margin on the edge of their wings	do not have a margin on the edge of their wings
have large, round compound eyes	have crescent-shaped compound eyes
do not have jaws	have jaws for biting
do not have a sting	have a sting

Hoverfly.

Common wasp.

Question 8 9 10 11 12

Centipede.

Millipede.

Check your progress

You should already know	Outcomes	Keywords

We often sort things into groups to make them easier to deal with. For example, the police have files containing millions of fingerprints. They use them to identify fingerprints found at crime scenes. If the fingerprints can be sorted into groups with similar **characteristics**, only one group of fingerprints needs to be checked, rather than all of them.

Whorls / Loops / Arches

whorl

Question 1

There are lots of ways of sorting living things. Some ways are more useful than others. We often start by sorting them into green plants and animals.

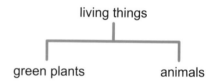

living things

green plants   animals

Question 2

Then we sort these groups into smaller groups. These pictures show one way of sorting animals into groups.

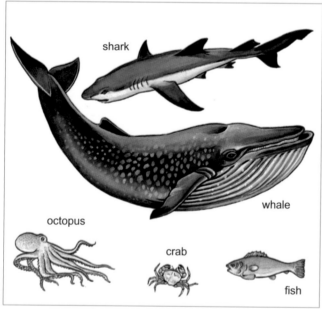

shark

whale

octopus

crab

fish

These animals live in water.

eagle

sparrow

bat

fly

owl

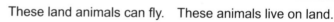

These land animals can fly.

badger

hamster

spider

cat

humans

horse

These animals live on land.

Question 3 **4** **5**

An ancient way of sorting

Aristotle lived in Greece over 2000 years ago. He was the first person to use sets of characteristics of animals and plants to sort them into groups.

Before Aristotle, people grouped animals into land and water animals or winged and wingless animals.

Aristotle saw that some ants have wings and others don't. So he realised that a simple grouping into winged and wingless animals doesn't work.

Aristotle (384–322 BC).

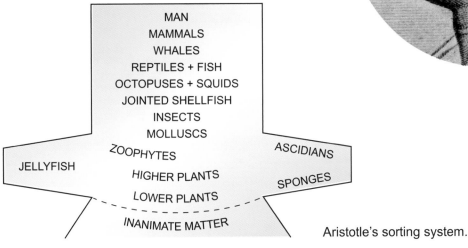

Aristotle's sorting system.

| Question 6 |

Sorting is useful

Birds have feathers but other animal groups don't. So feathers are a useful characteristic for identifying an animal as a bird. Also, birds have beaks and wings, and they walk on two legs. So if someone tells you that an eagle is a bird, you already know a lot of things about it.

You might see an animal that you haven't seen before but you recognise that it is a bird. So you look it up in a book about birds, rather than a book about all animals.

eagle

bat

dragonfly

Birds, bats and many insects fly. But bats and insects are very different from birds. So flying is not a useful characteristic for sorting animals.

| Question 7 |

You should already know	Outcomes	Keywords

Now we sort living things into groups that have lots of characteristics in common. Scientists all over the world use the same system. But it is not the same as Aristotle's system.

Scientists have named and described several million different species of plants and animals. They think that millions more will be discovered in the future. We can't learn about every one of them. So sorting is useful. We call this sorting **classification**.

A snail is an invertebrate with a shell.

Question 1	2	3

Classifying animals

When scientists find a new animal, they look at similarities and differences between it and known animals. Then they fit it into a group. Sometimes they have to change the groupings a bit.

Animals without backbones are called **invertebrates**. Some of them are soft bodied. Others have hard outer parts such as shells.

A crab is an invertebrate. Its jointed skeleton is on the outside of its body.

Question 4

Some animals have skeletons made of bone inside their bodies. We call them animals with backbones or **vertebrates**.

Question 5

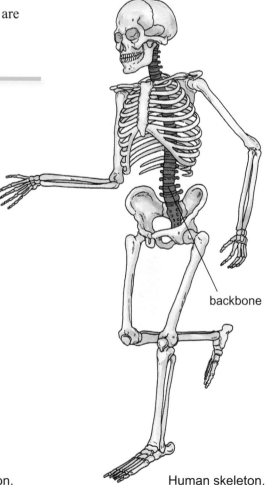

backbone

Human skeleton.

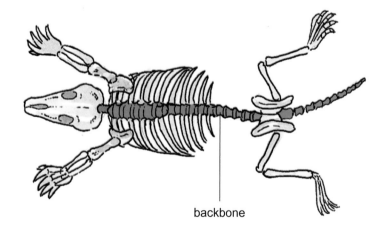

backbone

Mole skeleton.

Classifying vertebrates

There are about 60 000 different species of vertebrates that we know about, so we divide them into smaller groups.

Question 6 7 8 9

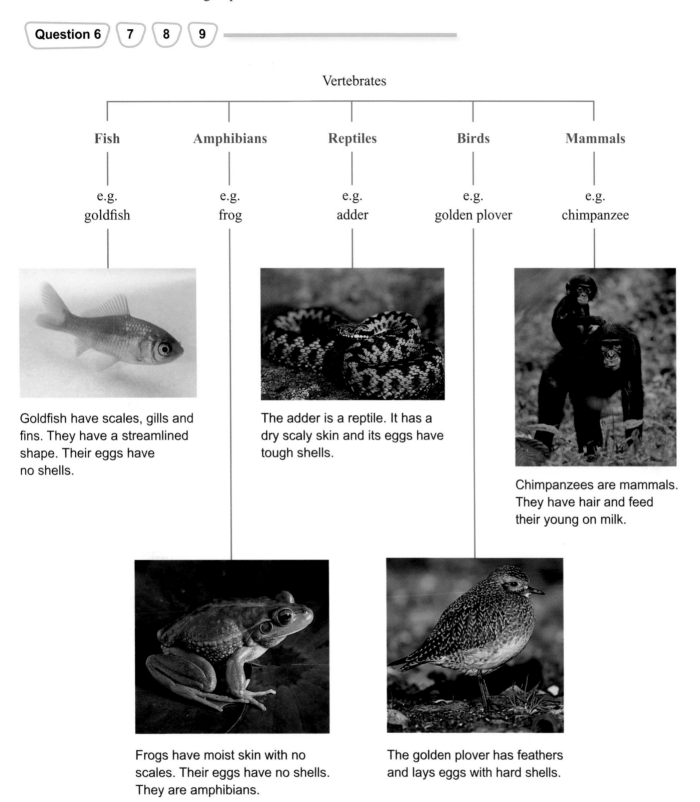

Vertebrates

| Fish | Amphibians | Reptiles | Birds | Mammals |

e.g. goldfish — e.g. frog — e.g. adder — e.g. golden plover — e.g. chimpanzee

Goldfish have scales, gills and fins. They have a streamlined shape. Their eggs have no shells.

The adder is a reptile. It has a dry scaly skin and its eggs have tough shells.

Chimpanzees are mammals. They have hair and feed their young on milk.

Frogs have moist skin with no scales. Their eggs have no shells. They are amphibians.

The golden plover has feathers and lays eggs with hard shells.

Invertebrates

Over nine-tenths of all species of animals don't have bones. They are
classified as invertebrates. We divide them into groups, too.

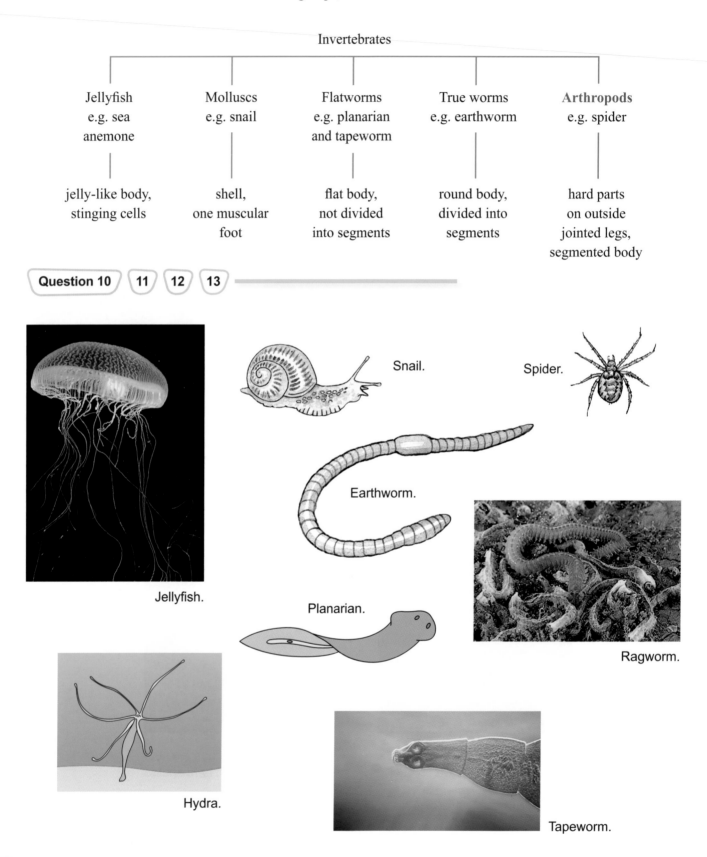

Invertebrates

Jellyfish e.g. sea anemone	Molluscs e.g. snail	Flatworms e.g. planarian and tapeworm	True worms e.g. earthworm	**Arthropods** e.g. spider
jelly-like body, stinging cells	shell, one muscular foot	flat body, not divided into segments	round body, divided into segments	hard parts on outside jointed legs, segmented body

Question 10 11 12 13

Jellyfish.

Snail.

Spider.

Earthworm.

Planarian.

Ragworm.

Hydra.

Tapeworm.

More groups

All the groups that we have studied so far are very big. So we divide them into smaller groups. More than three-quarters of all animal species are arthropods. We divide arthropods into four main groups.

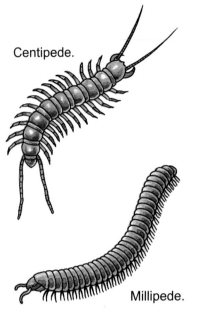

Centipede.

Crab.

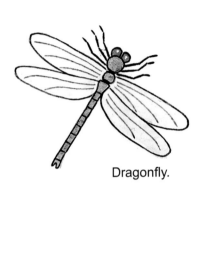

Dragonfly.

Fly.

Millipede.

Lobster.

Erigone.

Question 14 / **15** _____

Arthropod group	What do they look like?
crustaceans	two pairs of antennae; five or more pairs of legs
insects	three pairs of legs; one or two pairs of wings
spiders	four pairs of legs; no antennae
myriapods (many legs)	long body divided into segments; legs on every segment

Question 16 _____   **Review your work**

Summary ➡

You should already know

Outcomes

Keywords

Sorting information

You learned on page 42 that we sort things, including living things, into groups. We say that we **classify** them. This makes the information easier to deal with.

Look back at the diagram of Aristotle's **classification** system on page 43. Aristotle worked it out over 2000 years ago in ancient Greece. Notice that we still use some of his groupings.

Modern classification systems have their roots in the work of a Swedish scientist called Carl von Linne, also known as Linnaeus (1707–1778). At the start, his friend Peter Artedi (1705–1735) worked with him. However, Artedi died young so Linnaeus receives all the credit.

As well using the work of Aristotle, Ardeti and Linnaeus used ideas from

- Andrea Cesalpino (1519–1603), Italian
- John Ray (1627–1705), English
- Joseph Pitton de Tournefort (1656–1708), French

This is just one example of scientists building on the work of others – both from the past and from other cultures. As Isaac Newton said:

> If I have seen further it is by standing on the shoulders of giants.

Title page of Volume 1 of Linnaeus' *Systema Naturae*.

Question 1 **2**

Linnaeus' aim was to classify all **species**. At this time, people from Europe were exploring little known parts of the world. They were bringing back plants and animals that were unknown in Europe. Linnaeus wanted to create order out of the chaos of these collections by grouping together similar and related organisms into classes, orders, genera and species. Scientists from all of the developed world were able to use his system.

Question 3 **4**

Defining a species

You have considered a species as a group of living things that

- have similar characteristics
- can breed together and produce offspring that can also breed.

Recognising that two living things belong to the same species is not always easy. John Ray first defined a species.

The same but different (species)

Horses and donkeys are similar. They can breed to produce mules. But mules cannot breed. So horses and donkeys are different species.

Different but the same (species)

These dogs look very different. But they can interbreed. So they are the same species.

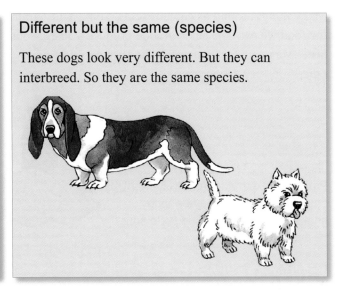

Naming species

Before Linnaeus, the naming of plants and animals was also muddled. The lengths of names varied and sometimes the same plant or animal was given a different name in different places.

Linnaeus worked out a system of using two names.

Look at the information in the box.

 Question 5 ⟨ 6 ⟩ ──────────────

Once a scientist has described and named a species, scientists around the world use the same Latin name. Locally, the name of the species stays the same.

Even within one country, the name of a plant or animal may vary. In different parts of the UK, the plant *Alliaria petiolata* is known as garlic mustard and Jack-by-the-hedge, as well as other names.

Question 7 ⟨ 8 ⟩ ──────────────

In Linnaeus' system, species have

- a generic name (of the **genus**)

- a specific name (of the species).

All humans alive now belong to the same species,
Homo sapiens.
(genus)   (species)

7E.1 What acids and alkalis are like (HSW)

You should already know

Outcomes

Keywords

Acids are all around us

Many things around us contain **acids**. Some acids are in the food we eat. The acids in food produce a sharp, sour taste. Many acids like those in food are harmless but others are very dangerous.

Fruit or drinks made from fruit often contain acids. They have a tangy, sharp taste. We say acids taste sour.

Question 1

In the 18th century sailors could be at sea for several years at a time. If they did not eat fresh fruit for a long time, they became ill with a disease called scurvy. Scurvy is caused by a lack of vitamin C in the diet. It can be fatal.

Captain Cook, who discovered Australia, made his sailors eat limes and lemons. This stopped them getting scurvy. In his three-and-a-half year trip to Australia, only one of his crew died of scurvy. This was amazing at the time. From then on, the British Navy made all its sailors drink lime juice to prevent scurvy. Even today, the nickname for British sailors is 'Limeys'.

Lime juice prevents scurvy because it contains vitamin C. Vitamin C is a weak acid so it tastes sour.

Lime juice tastes sour.

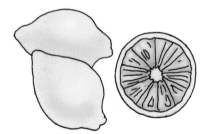

Limes and lemons taste sour because they contain citric acid. They prevent scurvy because they contain vitamin C. This is also an acid, but it is very weak.

Question 2

Some acids are dangerous

Fruit juice is not dangerous but there are some acids that are risky to use. Substances like **hydrochloric acid** have their own **hazard** warning sign. Hazard warning signs let people know that they need to be careful.

Hydrochloric acid is a **strong** acid that is **corrosive**. It will attack your skin and start eating it away.

This is the warning sign for corrosive.

CORROSIVE

Question 3

When you mix acid with water, we say that you **dilute** it. This makes the acid less dangerous. If you spill an acid, you should wash the area with lots of water to dilute the acid.

Dilute acids are still harmful. They will harm or irritate your skin even though they are not as dangerous as undiluted acids.

Many foods contain **weak** acids. Fruit juices and vinegar are examples. The weak acids in food can attack the surface of your teeth.

We use a black cross to warn people about them.

This is the sign for **harmful**.   This is the sign for **irritant**.

Question 4 5

About alkalis

The group of substances shown in the picture contain **alkalis**. When acids and alkalis react, their properties are cancelled out.

All these substances contain alkalis.

Some alkalis are safe to use. Others, such as **sodium hydroxide**, are just as dangerous as the strongest acids. They are also described as corrosive.

When you get alkali on your skin it dissolves your skin away. Your skin feels soapy and you get a chemical burn.

Many kitchen cleaners contain alkalis that attack grease.

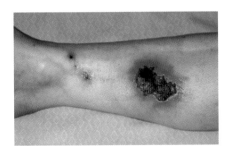

These burns were caused by an alkali called sodium hydroxide.

Question 6 7

| You should already know | Outcomes | Keywords |

Sodium hydroxide, hydrochloric acid, lemonade and water are all colourless liquids. They look the same, but they have a different effect on red cabbage juice, which shows that they are actually quite different.

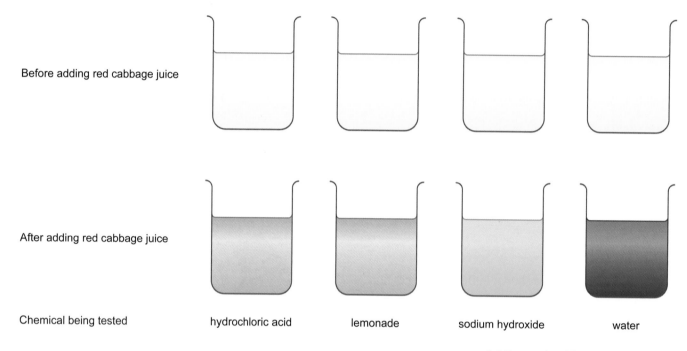

Before adding red cabbage juice

After adding red cabbage juice

Chemical being tested   hydrochloric acid   lemonade   sodium hydroxide   water

Adding red cabbage juice to four colourless liquids.

Question 1

We can use the colour change of red cabbage juice to show whether a substance is an acid or an alkali. We can use juices from some other plants too. We call plant juices <u>extracts</u>.

- Red cabbage juice and beetroot juice are vegetable extracts.
- Blackcurrant juice is a fruit extract.
- Litmus is extracted from a lichen.

These extracts show a different colour in acid to the one they show in alkali.

We call them **indicators**.

Question 2   **3**

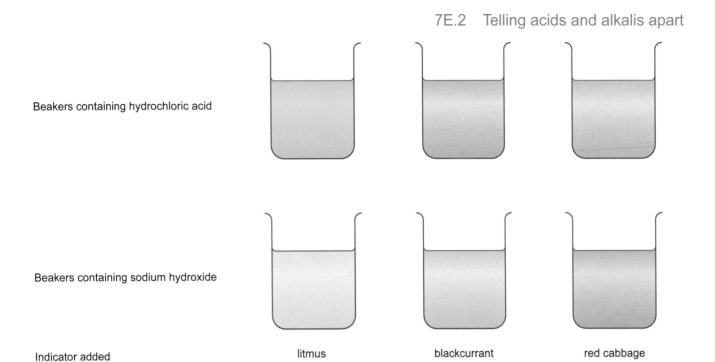

Beakers containing hydrochloric acid

Beakers containing sodium hydroxide

Indicator added

litmus   blackcurrant   red cabbage

The acid and alkali in the diagram have not been diluted very much. The colours show what happens when different substances are added to strong acid and strong alkali.

The colours of three indicators in acid and in alkali.

Question 4

Litmus is a dye. It is a very common indicator. It is purple when it is in a substance that is neither alkali nor acid. This type of substance is called a **neutral** substance.

Litmus turns red in acids. Litmus turns blue in alkalis. Water is neutral. It is neither acid nor alkali. Litmus turns purple in water.

Substance	Litmus colour	Type of substance
sodium hydroxide	blue	alkali
vitamin C	red	acid
water	purple	neutral
calcium hydroxide	blue	alkali
carbon dioxide	red	acid
hydrochloric acid	red	acid
potassium hydroxide	blue	alkali

Some examples of the colour of litmus in different substances.

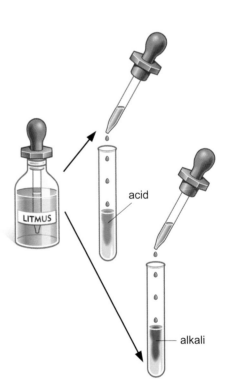

Question 5 6

You should already know   Outcomes   Keywords

We can use litmus to show if something is acidic, alkaline or neutral. We need a better indicator to show the difference between a strong acid like concentrated hydrochloric acid and a weak acid like lemon juice.

Universal indicator is a special type of indicator. You can use it to tell how strong or weak an acid or an alkali is. It is made by combining other indicators together.

Concentrated hydrochloric acid is a strong acid – it will attack your skin.

Lemonade is a weak acid – it does not damage skin.

Universal indicator shows different colours in these substances. We can also use it to tell whether an alkali is weak or strong.

strongly acidic

weakly acidic

neutral

weakly alkaline

strongly alkaline

Type of substance	Colour of litmus	Colour of universal indicator
strong acid	red	red
weak acid	red	yellow
neutral	purple	green
weak alkali	blue	blue
strong alkali	blue	purple

Question 1 2

The strengths of acids and alkalis are measured on a scale of numbers. This scale is called the **pH scale**. The scale goes from 0 to 14.

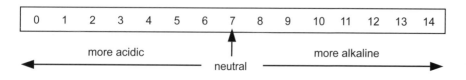

| 0 | 1 | 2 | 3 | 4 | 5 | 6 | 7 | 8 | 9 | 10 | 11 | 12 | 13 | 14 |

more acidic ← neutral → more alkaline   The pH scale.

Question 3

The different colours of universal indicator are matched to the numbers on the pH scale. When you buy universal indicator, you can buy a colour chart like this.

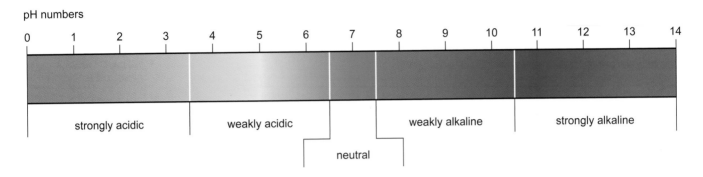

A colour chart for universal indicator that shows the pH scale.

On the pH scale, numbers between 0 and 3 tell us that the liquid is a strong acid. Hydrochloric acid is a strong acid. Acids with very low pH numbers carry the corrosive hazard sign.

The numbers 4 to 6 tell us that the liquid is a weak acid. Lemon juice is a weak acid.

Number 7 tells us that the liquid is neutral. Water has a pH of 7. It is neither acid nor alkali.

Numbers from 8 to 14 are for alkalis. Sodium hydroxide is a strong alkali. It has a pH of 14. Even dilute alkalis can be corrosive.

This chart shows what happens when you test some different substances with universal indicator.

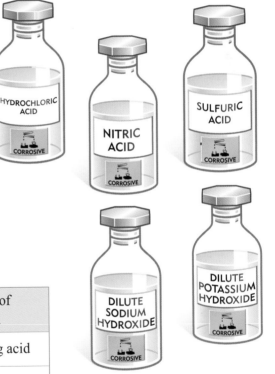

Hydrochloric acid, nitric acid and sulfuric acid are all acids. Sodium hydroxide and potassium hydroxide are alkalis. All of them are corrosive.

Liquid	Colour of universal indicator	pH	Type of liquid
nitric acid	red	1	strong acid
vinegar	yellow	5	weak acid
ammonia solution	purple	14	strong alkali
sodium bicarbonate solution	blue	9	weak alkali
salt water	green	7	neutral

Question 4 5 6

| You should already know | Outcomes | Keywords |

An acid **reacts** with an alkali to cancel it out. This reaction is called **neutralisation**.

When neutralisation happens, it produces a neutral substance called a **salt**. Water is also produced. The pH of the new substances is 7.

> acid + alkali → salt + water

As you add acid to an alkali, the pH falls from a high number. You have to add just the right amount of acid to the alkali to get a neutral solution. Too much acid will make the pH fall below 7 and give an acidic solution. Not enough acid will leave an alkali solution with a pH higher than 7.

IT STILL DOESN'T TASTE QUITE RIGHT!

<u>Never</u> do this to check whether the acid has gone!

Question 1 2

A neutralisation experiment

The diagram shows an experiment with hydrochloric acid, water and washing soda.

The washing soda crystal dissolves in the water around it, making it alkaline. A few drops of universal indicator has been added to the water. Then, some hydrochloric acid is carefully added to the top.

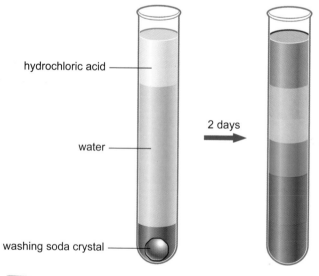

hydrochloric acid

water

2 days

washing soda crystal

Question 3 4

The photograph shows the experiment with hydrochloric acid, washing soda and water.

After a few days:

- the hydrochloric acid has moved slowly down the test tube;
- the washing soda crystal has dissolved in the water near it;
- the alkaline solution has moved up the test tube.

The universal indicator colour shows the change from acid to alkali as you go down the tube. There is a green band in the centre. The green band shows where the pH is 7 (in the photo, this is just under the yellow band). This is where neutralisation happens.

The experiment after a few days.

 Question 5 **6**

What happens to other acids and alkalis?

When an acid and an alkali neutralise each other, they produce a salt. The name of the salt depends on which acid and alkali are used.

> hydrochloric acid + sodium hydroxide → sodium chloride + water

The salt's name in this example is sodium chloride. Its first name is the same as the first name of the alkali. Its second name comes from the name of the acid.

- Sodium hydroxide gives <u>sodium</u>.
- Hydrochloric acid gives <u>chloride</u>.

This gives the salt the name <u>sodium chloride</u>.

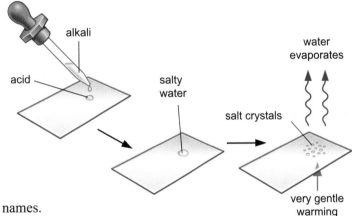

Different acids produce salts with different second names.

Acid used	Second name of salt
hydrochloric acid	chloride
nitric acid	nitrate
sulfuric acid	sulfate

If you add just the right amount of alkali to an acid, you can make the acid disappear.

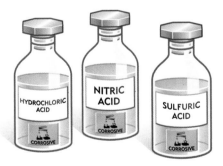

Question 7

Check your progress

You should already know | Outcomes | Keywords

Curing indigestion

Indigestion is caused by too much acid in the stomach. You can take medicine to neutralise this acid. Some indigestion medicines contains a weak alkali called magnesium hydroxide. This will neutralise excess stomach acid.

It is important that the alkali in the medicine is weak. If it is too strong, it will corrode your insides.

Some indigestion cures contain magnesium carbonate or sodium bicarbonate. Because these are carbonates, they react with the acid in your stomach to produce **carbon dioxide** gas. This is another way of neutralising the excess acid. Unfortunately, the gas produced can make you burp!

One of these is a medicine for indigestion.

Question 1 **2**

Here are the results of some tests with indigestion tablets.

Tablet	Cost per tablet	Amount of acid neutralised (cm³)	Amount of gas produced (cm³)	Time taken to neutralise the acid (minutes)
Brand A	3p	25	0	3
Brand B	4p	20	0	10
Brand C	5p	30	15	2
Brand D	1p	10	28	1
Brand E	8p	40	15	2

Question 3

Toothpaste

Your mouth is full of bacteria. These feed on bits of food left in your mouth. When bacteria feed they produce an acid. The acid can attack your teeth, making them decay.

When you brush your teeth you remove the bits of food and some of the bacteria. The toothpaste is also a weak alkali. The alkali in toothpaste neutralises the acid. This helps to protect your teeth. Sodium bicarbonate is a weak alkali that is commonly used in toothpaste.

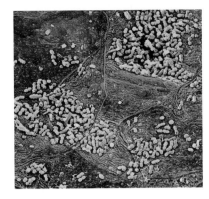

Bacteria on a human tongue.

The pH of this toothpaste is 8 because it contains sodium bicarbonate.

> Question 4

Making cakes rise

Baking powder is an ingredient in some cake recipes. It contains an acid and sodium bicarbonate (which is sometimes called bicarbonate of soda). The acid is called tartaric acid. When the cake is mixed, the liquid dissolves the acid and the sodium bicarbonate, and they react. Carbon dioxide gas is produced. The carbon dioxide gas makes the bubbles in sponge cakes. This is another type of neutralisation reaction because the products from the acid and the sodium bicarbonate reacting are neutral.

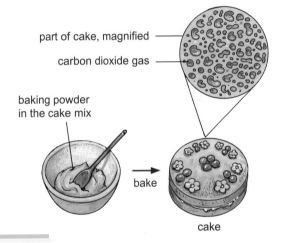

part of cake, magnified
carbon dioxide gas
baking powder in the cake mix
bake
cake

> Question 5

Acid rain

Pollution from factories and power stations produces acid gases in the air. Rainwater dissolves these acid gases so that its pH is lower than 7. Acid rain harms the environment. The water in rivers and lakes becomes slightly acidic. In Scandinavian countries, they add crushed limestone to their lakes to neutralise the acidity caused by acid rain.

The pH of soil is different in different places. Serious gardeners test their soil using universal indicator so they know its pH. Different plants grow best in different soils. In some areas, the soil is too acidic for any plants to grow well.

Lime is the common name for an alkali called calcium oxide. Farmers spread it on fields to neutralise some of the acid in the soil. Adding lime means that the pH of the soil is raised, making it less acidic. Plants can now grow well.

Calcium carbonate can be added to lakes to neutralise the water from acid rain.

> Review your work

> Summary ➡

> Question 6

You should already know | Outcomes | Keywords

Investigating the effect of temperature on a reaction

Some pupils are investigating whether the temperature of hydrochloric acid affects its reaction with a metal.

Group A adds some zinc to cold hydrochloric acid and some iron to some hot hydrochloric acid. Both test tubes produce bubbles of hydrogen gas at the same rate.

Group B sees what group A has done and decide that the test is not fair because they have used different metals – they cannot tell if the temperature is having an effect because the two metals might not react in the same way. Group B adds zinc to both cold and hot acid, and repeats the experiment with iron.

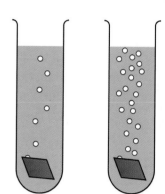

Zinc in cold acid and hot acid.

Question 1 2 3

The teacher explains to group A that their method does not give reliable evidence. This is because they have changed more than one thing at once when trying to compare the two test tubes.

When you make a judgement about how good or reliable an experiment is it is called **evaluation**.

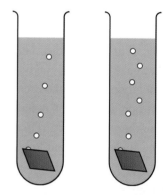

Iron in cold acid and hot acid.

Deciding what to do to make your method of working safe is called a **risk assessment**. The pupils in the diagram are wearing goggles but the bottles of acid are too close to the back edge of the desk. The pupil on the left is holding a test tube very close to his body. Both lab coats are open and not protecting the students very well at all if there is a spill. Both pupils are engrossed in their own activity and are not aware of what the other is doing.

Part of a risk assessment is to state what you would do to reduce the risk.

Question 4 5

Safety in science

When scientists plan investigations they need to think about:

- the plan of what to do;
- how to make any tests fair;
- the equipment and substances they use;
- safety.

You can look up **hazards** for different substances in books or on cards that are published about the substances. Some substances have hazard warning signs on their containers. In a risk assessment, you identify each hazard and decide what to do to reduce it.

CORROSIVE

This is the warning sign for corrosive.

This is the sign for **harmful**.

This is the sign for **irritant**.

Hazardous chemicals have warning labels. You need to be able to recognise them.

A funnel is used to fill a tube with hydrochloric acid.

A tube is used to put a measured amount of sodium hydroxide into a flask.

Some indicator is added to the flask.

The photographs show part of an experiment in which hydrochloric acid is added to sodium hydroxide. There are several safety features.

- The person is wearing goggles.
- The person is standing up.
- A funnel is used to direct the acid into a narrow tube.
- The substances used are clearly labelled.

Standing up is the result of a simple risk assessment. You can reduce the risk of spilling harmful chemicals on your legs if you stand up. If there is a spill on the worktop, it will drip onto the floor and not onto your lap.

Risk assessment is one part of science that affects the way people think and behave.

 Question 6   7

Even when you have done a risk assessment, accidents can happen. This might be because your risk assessment was not good enough. It might be because you are not following your risk assessment. It might just be due to some unexpected event, a pure accident.

Someone distracted this student during an experiment and she has spilled alkali onto her hand.

 Question 8   9

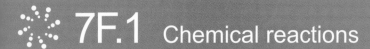

You should already know	Outcomes	Keywords

In a **chemical reaction**, new substances are made.

Chemical reactions happen everywhere. They happen when you cook food. They happen in your garden when plants grow. They happen inside your body to keep you alive.

If you heat an egg, the substances in it change into new substances. Once it is cooked, the egg will not go back to the way it was. We say a chemical reaction has happened. Chemical reactions make new substances.

A raw egg in a pan.

The cooked egg is hard and tastes different too.

Question 1

What else happens in a chemical reaction

Other things happen in a chemical reaction apart from getting a new substance. Sometimes there is a colour change. For example, this happens when iron reacts with **oxygen** in the air and rust is produced.

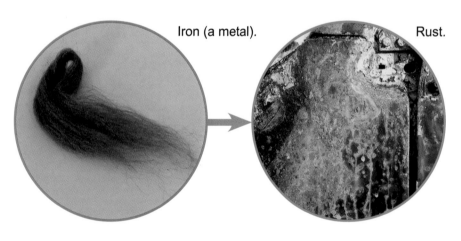

Iron (a metal).   Rust.

Sometimes the reaction will produce heat. This happens when a piece of potassium is put onto water. The reaction produces hydrogen gas and so much heat that the gas burns.

Potassium reacting with water.

Sometimes there is a change of pH. If you test the water after the potassium has reacted with it, you find a change of pH from neutral to alkaline.

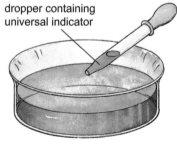

dropper containing universal indicator

The indicator turns purple, which shows that the solution is alkaline.

Question 2   **3**

Burning

When something burns, it reacts with the oxygen in the air. New substances are formed. **Burning** is an example of a chemical reaction. Another word for burning is combustion. One of the new substances formed is usually a type of substance called an **oxide**.

The proper name for natural gas is **methane**. When methane burns in a Bunsen burner, it produces a new gas called carbon dioxide.

Question 4

You can describe burning with a **word equation** like this:

substance + oxygen → substance oxide

Burning natural gas in air.

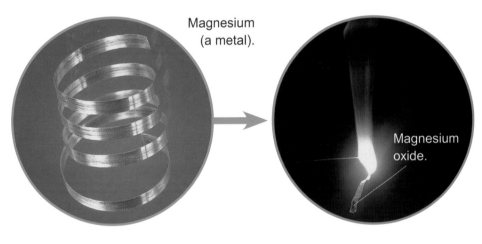

Magnesium (a metal).

Magnesium oxide.

When magnesium burns, it reacts with the oxygen in the air. The word equation that describes this is:

magnesium + oxygen → magnesium oxide

Magnesium oxide is a white, powdery solid.

When carbon burns, it produces a gas called carbon dioxide. Not all oxides are solids.

The word equation to describe this reaction is:

carbon + oxygen → carbon dioxide

Carbon dioxide.

Carbon (a non-metal).

Question 5 **6**

You should already know | Outcomes | Keywords

The pictures show two experiments.

In the first experiment, magnesium reacts with hydrochloric acid. A gas is produced. The gas is **hydrogen**. It is a new substance. This means that magnesium reacting with hydrochloric acid is a chemical reaction.

When the acid is added to the magnesium, the piece of magnesium gradually gets smaller. It eventually disappears. This is an example of **corrosion**. The liquid in the tube at the end is a new substance. It is a solution of magnesium chloride. If you let the hydrogen gas escape from the tube and leave the tube open so the solution evaporates then solid magnesium chloride is left behind.

In the first experiment, magnesium and hydrochloric acid react together. We call them **reactants**.

The new substances produced are hydrogen and magnesium chloride. We call them **products**.

You can describe the first reaction with a word equation like this:

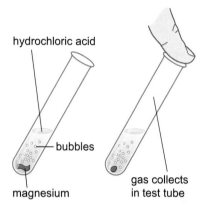

hydrochloric acid
bubbles
magnesium
gas collects in test tube

magnesium + hydrochloric acid → magnesium chloride + hydrogen

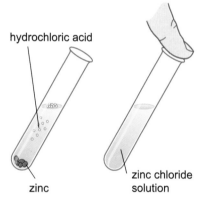

hydrochloric acid
zinc
zinc chloride solution

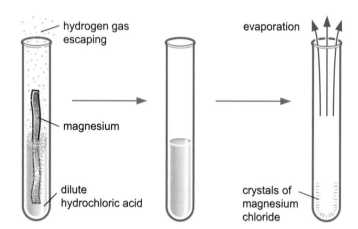

hydrogen gas escaping

magnesium

dilute hydrochloric acid

evaporation

crystals of magnesium chloride

The reactants are on the left. The products are on the right. The arrow shows the way the reaction goes.

reactants → products

Question 1

When magnesium or zinc react with an acid, one of the products is hydrogen. The other new material that is made is called a **salt**.

To make the salt called magnesium chloride you react magnesium with hydrochloric acid. You add more magnesium than you need to make sure all the acid is used up.

You then filter off the left-over magnesium when the reaction is finished.

The products are water and magnesium chloride.

The magnesium chloride is dissolved in the water so you need to evaporate it to get the salt magnesium chloride.

Metal	Acid	Salt
magnesium	hydrochloric acid	magnesium chloride
zinc	hydrochloric acid	zinc chloride
iron	hydrochloric acid	iron chloride
magnesium	sulfuric acid	magnesium sulfate

Different combinations of metals and acids make different salts.

When zinc and hydrochloric acid react, the products are hydrogen gas and zinc chloride solution. The zinc chloride gets its first name from zinc because it was the metal used. It gets its second name from the acid used, which was hydrochloric acid.

The word equation for the reaction is:

zinc + hydrochloric acid → zinc chloride + hydrogen

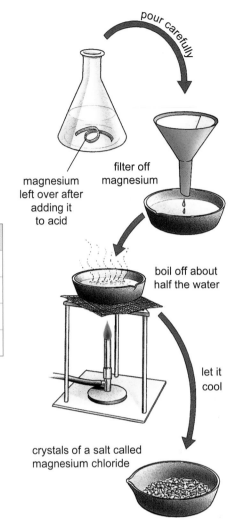

pour carefully

magnesium left over after adding it to acid

filter off magnesium

boil off about half the water

let it cool

crystals of a salt called magnesium chloride

Question 4 **5**

The test for hydrogen gas is shown in the picture. Hydrogen gas burns with a squeaky pop. To test it you light a splint and put it to the mouth of the test tube. When the hydrogen pops, it is reacting with oxygen in the air to make water.

hydrogen + oxygen → water

Hydrogen gas is a lot lighter than air. You need to keep a finger or thumb over the test tube to trap the gas before you test it.

When you test for hydrogen you have to move your thumb or finger at the same moment as you put the splint to the tube or the hydrogen will escape. If it escapes, there will be no hydrogen to test!

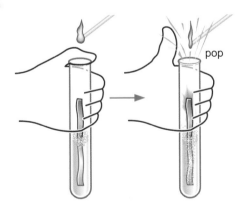

pop

hydrogen + oxygen → water

Testing hydrogen gas with a lighted splint.

Question 6

You should already know

Outcomes

Keywords

Many of the rocks in the Earth contain substances called **carbonates**. Geologists use acid to test rocks to see if they contain carbonates. If a rock contains carbonates then it will fizz and produce a gas called **carbon dioxide** when you put acid on it.

Chalk.

Limestone.

Marble.

The top pictures show three different types of rock, all made from calcium carbonate. Limestone is fairly hard and used as a building material. Chalk is soft and can be rubbed away easily. It is sometimes used to write with. Marble can be polished and is used as a decorative rock in buildings.

Hydrochloric acid will react with any of these three rocks and produce carbon dioxide gas because they are all made from a carbonate.

Washing soda and baking powder are household substances that contain carbonates. Vinegar has a pH of 5, which means that it is acidic. If you add vinegar to washing soda or baking powder then they will fizz and produce carbon dioxide.

Carbon dioxide gas is given off.

Question 1 2

The air always contains a very small amount of carbon dioxide. In recent years, this has been increasing because of the fuels we burn. When people talk about their 'carbon footprint', they are referring to the things they do that add to the carbon dioxide in the air. These might be things like travelling on an aircraft or using a car, both of which burn fuel.

Carbon dioxide reacts with rainwater to make a very weak acid. Over years and years, this acid can damage buildings as well as living things growing in the Earth's surface.

Some buildings are made from limestone. These are easily damaged when the acid in the rain reacts with the limestone. The photographs show the effect on York Minster. After hundreds of years of weak acid attacking the limestone, it needs to be restored to what it was like when it was built.

Stonework on York Minster before (left) and after (right) restoration.

Question 3

Carbon dioxide is an important gas. It is not only produced by the reaction between an acid and a carbonate. It is also produced when things burn. Living things produce carbon dioxide during **respiration**. The test for carbon dioxide is different from the test for hydrogen.

If you test carbon dioxide with a lighted splint, it puts the splint out. It does not make a squeaky pop. There are other gases that will put a lighted splint out so this is not a good test for carbon dioxide.

Lime water is a clear liquid. If you bubble carbon dioxide through lime water, the lime water goes cloudy. Carbon dioxide is the only gas that does this. It reacts with the lime water and produces calcium carbonate, a new substance. Calcium carbonate does not dissolve in water so it appears as very tiny white particles. To the naked eye this makes the lime water looks cloudy.

When you breathe out, your breath contains more carbon dioxide than the air you breathe in. This is because the cells in your body make carbon dioxide as part of the living processes called respiration. Carbon dioxide is a waste product so your body gets rid of it. You can test this with a straw and some lime water. Bubbling our breath through lime water will turn the lime water cloudy.

lime water

Carbon dioxide makes lime water go cloudy.

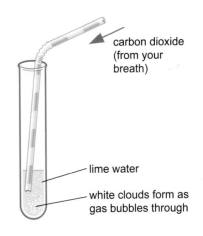

carbon dioxide (from your breath)

lime water

white clouds form as gas bubbles through

Question 4   5

Using carbonates at home

To make light fluffy cakes, you need to get small bubbles inside the cake as it cooks. One way of doing this is to use a substance called baking powder in the recipe.

Baking powder is a mixture of two white powders called tartaric acid and sodium bicarbonate. They don't react when they are dry.

When you use baking powder in a cake mix, it gets wet and the tartaric acid and sodium bicarbonate react. They produce small bubbles of carbon dioxide gas in the cake mixture. The bubbles of gas are a new substance that is made because a chemical reaction has happened.

As the cake cooks, the trapped bubbles get bigger and make the cake light and fluffy.

Another way of doing the same thing is to use self-raising flour in a cake. This is flour that has some baking powder already added to it so that it will make carbon dioxide bubbles in the cake mixture.

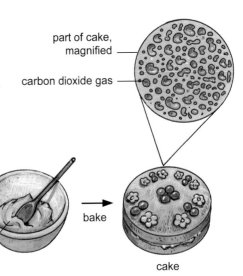

part of cake, magnified

carbon dioxide gas

baking powder in the cake mix

bake

cake

Question 6   7

Check your progress

You should already know

Outcomes

Keywords

Fuels

We burn some substances because they produce heat. We call them **fuels**.

You need three things to make a fire:

- a fuel;
- oxygen from the air;
- heat to get the fuel burning.

When the fire is lit, it produces light and more heat.

We can think of the three things needed for a fire as the sides of a triangle. When you take away one of the sides the fire goes out. This idea is used in fire fighting. The triangle is known as the **fire triangle**.

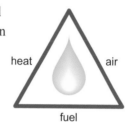

Fire-fighters use water to cool substances.

 Question 1 2

Some fuels come from the remains of plants and animals that died millions of years ago. We call them **fossil fuels**. Examples are coal, gas, oil and petrol. These fuels are rich in carbon compounds. When you burn a fossil fuel, the products are carbon dioxide and water.

The word equation for burning a fossil fuel is:

fossil fuel + oxygen → carbon dioxide + water

Fossil fuels are made from carbon and hydrogen. We call them hydrocarbons. A common fossil fuel is natural gas. The chemical name for natural gas is **methane**. This is the gas used in Bunsen burners and domestic cookers.

The word equation for methane burning is:

methane + oxygen → carbon dioxide + water

Fire extinguishers often contain carbon dioxide. This smothers the fire by keeping out the air.

 Question 3 4

Burning natural gas in air.

Wax is a fuel that is also made from hydrogen and carbon. A candle uses wax as its fuel. Wax is a solid. It has to be turned into a gas before it will burn. Another word for the gas you get from heating something is a vapour. When you light a candle:

- the heat from the flame melts the wax;
- the wick soaks up the molten wax;
- the flame turns the molten wax into wax vapour;
- the wax vapour mixes with air and burns;
- this produces carbon particles that glow yellow in the heat;
- as more air mixes in, the carbon also burns.

You can put a candle out by covering it with a jar. The candle burns for about half a minute. The flame then gets weaker and goes out.

The candle goes out because it has used up the oxygen inside the jar and produced carbon dioxide.

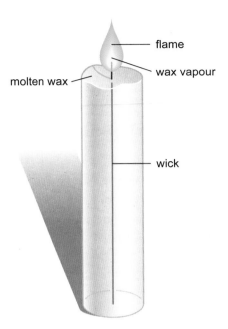

flame

wax vapour

molten wax

wick

At first the candle continues to burn.

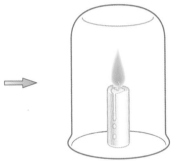

After about 20 seconds the candle is still burning.

After about 30 seconds the candle goes out.

To start with, the jar is full of air. Air is a mixture of gases. There is 21% oxygen and the rest is mostly nitrogen with a little bit of carbon dioxide and argon. Nitrogen, carbon dioxide and argon do not take part in burning. If there is no oxygen or if oxygen cannot get to a flame then it will go out.

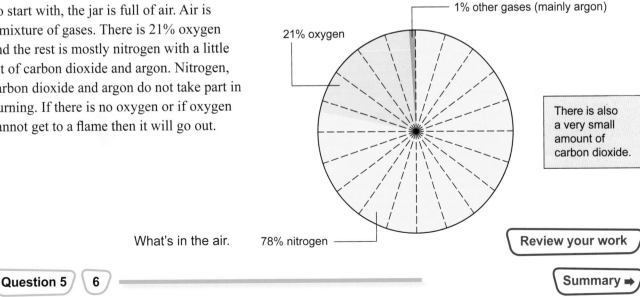

1% other gases (mainly argon)

21% oxygen

There is also a very small amount of carbon dioxide.

What's in the air.   78% nitrogen

Review your work

Summary ➡

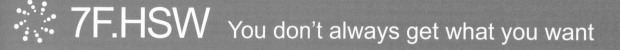

You should already know | Outcomes | Keywords

Measuring how fast a reaction happens

If you add magnesium to dilute acid, hydrogen gas is produced. If you attach a large syringe to the top of the apparatus so that the hydrogen cannot escape, it will push the syringe back and you can measure how much gas is produced at different times in the experiment.

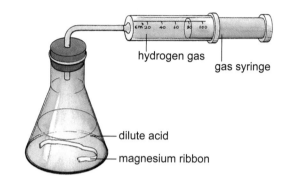

hydrogen gas

gas syringe

dilute acid

magnesium ribbon

You might get a set of results like this from the experiment shown in the diagram.

Just by looking at the results in the table you can see that, after 4 minutes, the reaction has finished.

Question 1 / 2

If you want to look at the results more carefully you can plot a graph. The graph shows a surprising result at 1.5 minutes. The volume of gas produced does not fit into the pattern of results.

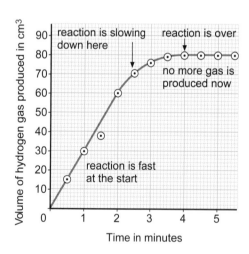

Time (minutes)	Total volume of gas produced (cm³)
0	0
0.5	15
1	30
1.5	38
2	60
2.5	70
3	76
3.5	79
4	80
4.5	80
5	80

When scientists get unexpected results like this, they go back and check them. These results are usually just mistakes or **errors**. They are called **anomalous** results. A result like this could be caused by reading the scale on the syringe incorrectly. The graph helps you spot anomalous results.

Question 3 / 4

Surprising results are not always wrong

Sometimes the result of an experiment is surprising but not an error.

If you do the experiment shown in the diagram very carefully, you will get a result that is a surprise to many people. After the magnesium has burned, the ash left is heavier than the magnesium was to start with!

This type of observation was made in 1772 by the important French chemist Antoine Lavoisier. At the time, everyone expected the ashes from something that burned to be lighter. This seemed obvious because:

- ashes are usually smaller than the substance that burned;
- flames have been seen escaping from the substance so it looks like something has left the original material.

Lavoisier worked out that the ashes being heavier was not a mistake. He did experiments for years with different substances to test his ideas. In 1779 he proposed that, when something burned, it combined with a gas that was in the air. This explained why the ash was heavier. Burning was not something escaping from the substance – it was something combining with it.

He also worked out that the part of the air taking part in burning was the part we use up in respiration. He gave it the name <u>oxygen</u>.

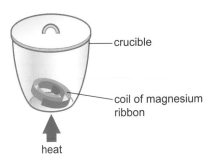

crucible

coil of magnesium ribbon

heat

When we heat magnesium in air, we have to lift the lid to allow oxygen in.

 Question 5

Accidental discoveries with sweet results

Sometimes, a scientist will notice something by accident and discover something important. In 1879, two chemists working in the USA, Ira Rensen and Constantin Fahlberg, accidentally discovered a substance that was 300 times sweeter than sugar and that does not make you put on weight like sugar does. It is called saccharin and we use it today as an artificial sweetener in many foods.

There is some controversy over what happened. Fahlberg claimed he spilt the substance on his hand and accidentally licked it. Rensen claimed he forgot to wash his hands after work and noticed that a bread roll he was eating later tasted very sweet. Whatever the truth was, the discovery of saccharin as a sweetener was not planned!

The discovery of the sweetener sucralose is even more bizarre. This was accidentally discovered in the 1970s by a researcher who mistook the word 'testing' for 'tasting'!

Antoine Lavoisier lived during the French Revolution. It was a time when many old ideas and theories were challenged.

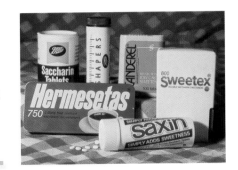

 Question 6 **7**

7G.1 Looking at substances (HSW)

All the substances we can see and feel in the world are called **matter**. Examples include gold, leaves, brick, air and water. There are millions of examples of different types of matter.

To make it easier to study and understand the world, scientists sort things into groups. Then they divide large groups into other, smaller groups.

Scientists sort substances into the groups **solid**, **liquid** and **gas**. Scientists call these three groups the three **states of matter**.

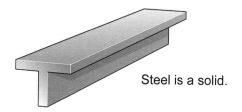

Steel is a solid.

Nitrogen dioxide is a brown gas.

Meths is a purple liquid.

Question 1

Solids have a definite shape and volume. They are very difficult to squash. Some solids seem to be heavy for their size – we say that they are dense. Steel is a good example of a solid.

Liquids take up the shape of the container they are in up to the level they fill it to. They keep the same volume. They are difficult to squash. Liquids can flow, which means they can be poured and can move through gaps. Generally, liquids aren't very heavy for their size.

Gases fill any container. Gases flow like liquids. They are very easy to squash. Most gases are light for their size.

A suitcase full of air is a lot lighter than one full of gold!

Solids		Liquids		Gases at 20 °C in a normal room	
Substance	Mass	Substance	Mass	Substance	Mass
iron	7 g	water	1 g	air	0.0013 g
gold	18 g	olive oil	0.9 g	oxygen	0.0014 g
pine	0.5 g	petrol	0.9 g	carbon dioxide	0.0019 g
cork	0.2 g	fruit cordial	1.3 g	hydrogen	0.00009 g

The masses of a cubic centimetre of some different substances.

Question 2 | 3

Matter behaves in a lot of different ways. Scientists try to explain why matter behaves in the ways it does.

Some observations of the way matter behaves are that:

- liquids and gases will flow but solids will not;
- substances can change from liquid to solid if they get cold enough;
- liquids like water change into a gas if you heat them;
- you can smell some substances like perfume and air freshener from across a room;
- some substances, like a tube of gas, can be squashed;
- some substances get bigger when you heat them;
- some substances can be stretched and then spring back;
- some substances are heavier than others.

On a snowy day, Sadia gets her milk from the doorstep.

It is cold and the top of the milk is frozen solid.

Sadia cannot pour the milk because the top is frozen.

Question 4

Scientists collect observations about matter. They think of ideas to explain the observations. We call these ideas **theories**.

Scientists discuss their theories and argue about them. They don't always agree. The scientists often need to look for more observations. They try to see if their theory explains the new evidence. If it doesn't, they change their theory or even make a new theory altogether.

The best theory we have that explains observations of matter uses the idea of <u>particles</u>.

Scientists think that everything is made up of a range of very tiny particles arranged in different ways in solids, liquids and gases.

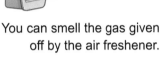

Some substances can be squashed.

You can smell the gas given off by the air freshener.

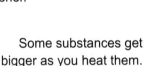

Some substances get bigger as you heat them.

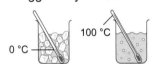

Some substances are heavier than others.

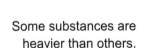

Scientists discuss and argue about ideas all the time.

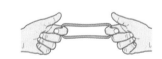

Some substances get longer.

Question 5 **6**

7G.2 The particle theory

Scientists think all matter is made from very small **particles**. This is a very old idea. Over 2000 years ago in ancient Greece, a scientist called Democritus thought that everything was made of small particles.

Democritus imagined that he had a bar of gold and a magic knife. The magic knife could cut any substance. When he cut the bar of gold in half, the two halves were smaller than the whole bar. As he kept cutting, the pieces got smaller and smaller. He thought that eventually he would get a very small particle that the knife would not cut.

The particles are too small to see with a microscope but you can get a picture of them using a beam of tiny particles called electrons.

Breaking down substances always makes particles.

Question 1

The theory changed until it had five main ideas. The theory was based on a picture of the tiny particles being a bit like snooker balls. These five ideas and the pictures that go with them are called the **particle model of matter**.

1 All matter is made up of particles.
2 The particles can be of different sizes.
3 The particles move around by themselves.
4 The particles attract each other.
5 The hotter the substance, the faster the particles move.

The word <u>kinetic</u> means <u>to do with movement</u>. Because the particle model of matter uses the idea of moving particles, it is also called the **kinetic theory**.

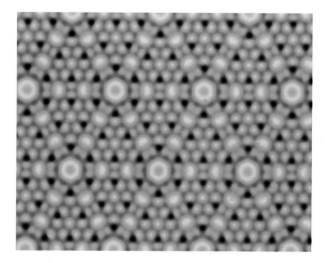

A photograph of particles from a crystal of silicon. This photograph was taken using an electron beam.

A 1 cm³ cube of air contains about 30 million million million particles (30×10^{18}).

1 cm

Question 2 3

Particles in solids, liquids and gases

Solids, liquids and gases are all made up of particles.

In solids, forces of attraction hold the particles together. The particles **vibrate**. This means that they shake quickly from side to side, but they don't change place with the particles next to them. There is very little space between the particles. This is why solids are harder than liquids and can stay in one shape.

In liquids, the particles still vibrate. They are almost as close together as they are in a solid but they can swap places with each other. The particles in a liquid are always moving about. The force of attraction between them is a bit less than it is in a solid. This is why liquids can be poured and why it is easy to push something into a liquid.

Because the particles in a liquid are still close together, it is hard to squash a liquid.

The particles in a gas are far apart, a long way from each other. They fly about freely, bouncing off each other and anything in their way, like the walls of the container they are in. There is very little attraction between the particles and they move very fast. A typical oxygen particle in the air on a summer's day will be moving at about 500 metres per second! This is why gases spread out and fill any space.

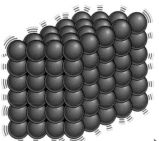

In solids, the particles vibrate while staying in their places.

In liquids, the particles still vibrate. They are attracted to each other less than in a solid. This means that they can swap places with each other.

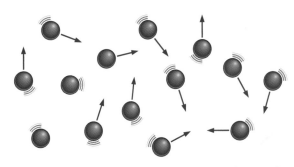

Gases spread out to fill their container.

> **Question 4** **5**

Because the particles in a gas are spread out, it is easy to squash a gas.

One of the main differences between solids, liquids and gases is that solids cannot flow. Liquids and gases can flow, and gases are able to spread into any space. The drawing shows how the particle model explains this.

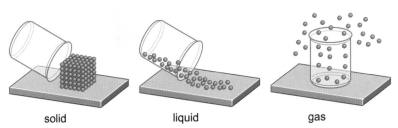

solid   liquid   gas

Solids cannot flow. Liquids and gases can flow. Gases can spread out.

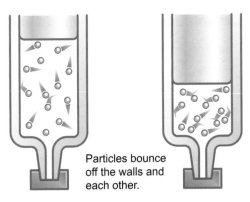

Particles bounce off the walls and each other.

A gas is mostly empty space, so you can squeeze the particles into a smaller space.

> **Question 6** **7**

> **Check your progress**

You should already know

Outcomes

Keywords

Particles in crystals

Many solids are made up of crystals. Crystals have straight edges. The idea of particles can be used to explain this.

The photograph shows some copper sulfate crystals. The diagram shows how scientists think the particles in copper sulfate line up to make the crystals.

Look at the straight edges of these crystals.

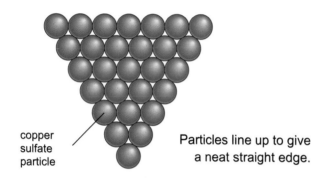

copper sulfate particle

Particles line up to give a neat straight edge.

Because all the copper sulfate particles are the same size and shape, they stick together in a block like a pack of snooker balls. Even though each of them is round, the pack has straight edges.

Question 1

Compressing solids, liquids and gases

Compressing means squashing. If you trap a solid, a liquid and a gas inside a plunger, there is a difference when you try to squash them. Solids and liquids are very difficult to compress. They do not squash easily. Gases are easy to compress. We can use the particle model to explain this.

This idea is used in car safety. An air bag will inflate in front of the driver in a crash. The driver hits a cushion of air that squashes, rather than hitting the hard steering wheel.

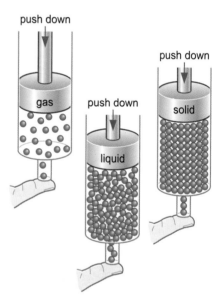

Only gases have enough space between their particles to allow them to be squashed a lot when you compress them.

Question 2

Melting, boiling, freezing and condensing

We use heat to melt a solid. Heat makes the particles vibrate faster. When the particles get enough energy, they start to overcome the attractive forces between them. The particles can then start to swap places – the solid starts **melting** to form a liquid.

If we continue to heat the particles, they get even more energy and move faster still. The particles break free from each other and a gas is formed. You have made the liquid begin **evaporating**. If you heat it enough, the evaporation makes bubbles inside the liquid. We call this boiling.

Condensing is the name for a gas changing to a liquid. **Freezing** is the name for a liquid changing to a solid. The clouds coming from a kettle are the steam condensing to water droplets in the cooler air.

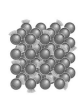 melting boiling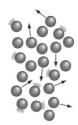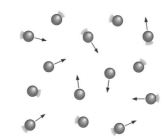
freezing condensing

Question 3 4

Some things are heavier than others

Solid	Mass in grams
lead	11.4
steel	7.7
aluminium	2.7
brass	8.5

Some substances are heavier than others.

The masses of 1 centimetre cubes of some different metals.

A cubic centimetre of aluminium is a lot lighter than a cubic centimetre of the other metals shown in the table. The particle model explains this by saying that the individual particles in aluminium are lighter than the particles in the other metals. This makes a block of aluminium lighter than similar blocks of the other metals. Metals like aluminium are used in racing bicycles to keep them as light as possible.

Another idea is that particles of some substances are packed together more tightly than others. A combination of these ideas explains why some substances are heavier than others.

Question 5

You should already know   Outcomes   Keywords

Diffusion

Look at the pictures. They show how some liquids and gases seem to spread out without any help from air currents, water currents or stirring. We call this spreading out **diffusion**.

You can see diffusion in a liquid if you put a drop of ink into some still water. You can also use a coloured crystal that will dissolve in the water. Once the ink or crystal has settled down, the colour spreads very slowly through the water. It sometimes takes a few weeks!

The same effect happens with a gas but much more quickly. This is because gas particles have a lot of space between each other and fly about very fast. The brown gas and the air in the diagram will spread into the whole space in about 10 minutes.

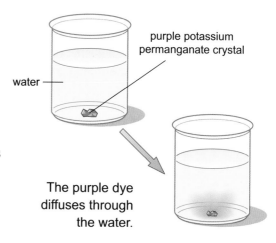

purple potassium permanganate crystal

water

The purple dye diffuses through the water.

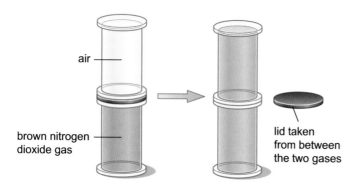

air

brown nitrogen dioxide gas

lid taken from between the two gases

The gases spread out.

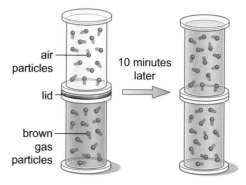

air particles

10 minutes later

lid

brown gas particles

The gas particles are moving, so they mix. We say that they diffuse.

Question 1

Hydrochloric acid produces a gas. So does ammonia. These two gases react when they meet and form a white solid. The product is a white substance called ammonium chloride.

If you set up this experiment, you can explain it with the idea of diffusion. You can explain why the ammonium chloride forms where it does if you know that ammonia gas particles move twice as fast as particles of hydrogen chloride gas.

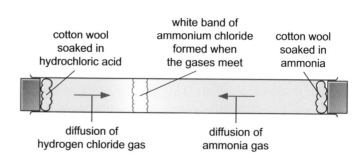

cotton wool soaked in hydrochloric acid

white band of ammonium chloride formed when the gases meet

cotton wool soaked in ammonia

diffusion of hydrogen chloride gas

diffusion of ammonia gas

The two transparent gases diffuse. They form a white cloud when they meet. Both of the gases have particles that are moving.

Question 2   3

Crushing a can

If you heat a can containing a little water, the water boils and the steam drives out most of the air from inside the can. If you put the lid back on the can and leave it to cool, it will collapse.

- The steam forces out the air particles that were inside the can.
- Because the top is put back on, the air cannot get back inside the can when the steam condenses.
- The force of the particles on the outside crushes the can because it is greater than the force of the particles on the inside.

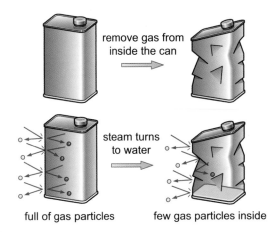

remove gas from inside the can

steam turns to water

full of gas particles   few gas particles inside

The can is crushed because more particles are hitting the outside than the inside of the can.

Question 4

Heat conduction in solids

A spoon gets hot because heat travels through the metal of the spoon. Particles at high temperatures vibrate faster than those at lower temperatures. The faster particles make their slower neighbours vibrate faster too. The faster vibrations pass through the spoon and eventually the top of the spoon gets hot. We call this **conduction** of heat.

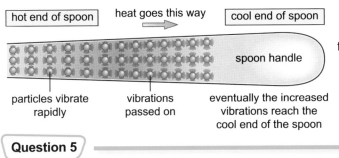

hot end of spoon   heat goes this way   cool end of spoon

spoon handle

particles vibrate rapidly

vibrations passed on

eventually the increased vibrations reach the cool end of the spoon

The faster vibrations are passed along the spoon. Heat travels through the metal. This is called conduction of heat.

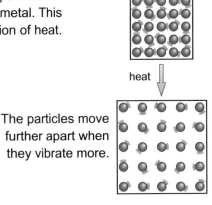

heat

The particles move further apart when they vibrate more.

Question 5

Expansion means getting bigger. Most substances expand when you heat them. Solids expand slightly, liquids expand more and gases expand a lot.

When a substance expands, the particles speed up and move further apart. They take up more space. This effect is used in thermometers filled with mercury. Mercury is a liquid metal. When the temperature goes up, the mercury expands and moves up the scale to show a higher temperature.

Heating the liquid in the boiling tube causes it to expand. The liquid moves up the tube.

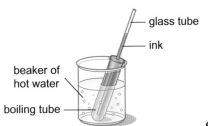

glass tube

ink

beaker of hot water

boiling tube

holder

iron bar

When the solid bar is heated it expands. It no longer fits the holder.

flask containing air

A little warmth from a pair of hands makes the air expand. The air bubbles out of the tube.

water

Review your work

Question 6

Summary ➡

You should already know   Outcomes   Keywords

What is Brownian motion?

Bits of dust or smoke particles are so small and light that they float about suspended in air. Pollen grains are also small and light: if you mix them in water, they float about like dust does in the air.

If you look at dust in air or pollen in water through a microscope, you see something very strange. The dust or pollen grains are jiggling about in a random way. They are constantly moving in a zigzag manner.

This was first noticed by a Scottish biologist called Robert Brown, in 1827. It is called **Brownian motion**.

Robert Brown (1773–1858).

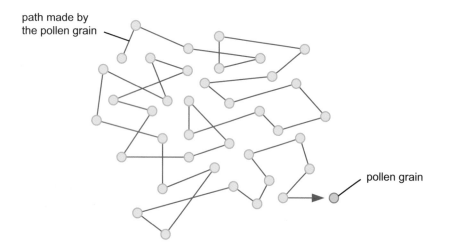

The path of a pollen grain that is jiggling about.

Testing an explanation

Robert Brown tried to explain what he saw but he failed.

His first idea was that the pollen grains were still alive because they had come from a plant, and that that made them move

He tested this idea. He looking at some water trapped in a lump of transparent rock called quartz. The water had been trapped in the quartz for millions of years. When he looked at the water, it had bits in that were jiggling about just like the pollen grains.

These bits could not be alive because they had been trapped in the quartz for far too long. Brown's second observation showed his explanation could not be the correct one.

Question 1   2   3

More observations

Over the next 70 years or so, other scientists from other countries and other branches of science made different observations of Brownian motion.

By 1900, people knew that:

- the speed of Brownian motion depends on the size of the particle – small particles jiggle faster than larger ones;
- particles jiggled faster if the liquid or gas they were in was hotter;
- there is no pattern to the jiggling – it is random.

These observations fitted in with the **particle model of matter**, which was being worked out from about 1870 onwards.

In the particle model of matter, a fluid like air or water is made up of millions of invisible particles that are always moving. This means that dust or pollen particles jiggle about because they are being knocked about by the invisible particles of air or water. The diagram shows the idea.

A 1 cm³ cube of air contains about 30 million million million particles (3 × 10¹⁹).

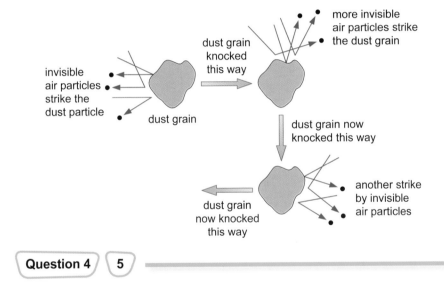

 **Question 4** / 5

A dust grain is hit by invisible air particles, making it jiggle about in a random way.

Albert Einstein

In 1905, Albert Einstein worked out a mathematical theory about Brownian motion that could be tested by experiment. Tests showed his ideas worked. The results allowed scientists to work out the sizes and masses of the invisible particles that make up matter.

Using Einstein's explanation, a French scientist called Jean Perrin was able to calculate how many invisible particles make up an element like oxygen once you know how many grams of oxygen you have.

This is an example of overlap between mathematics, physics and chemistry, all following from an observation by a biologist.

Question 6 / 7

Albert Einstein, mathematician and physicist (1879–1955).

You should already know ⟩ Outcomes ⟩ Keywords ⟩

If you spill water on an exercise book the ink might 'run' but the pencil doesn't. This is because water **dissolves** some types of ink but does not dissolve pencil.

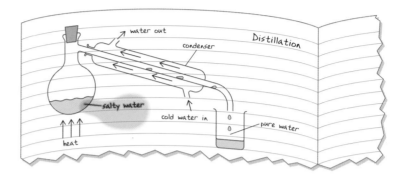

If you mix salt into a beaker of water, the salt seems to vanish.
If you mix sand into a beaker of water, the sand just sinks to the bottom.

Both the beakers now contain a **mixture** of a solid and a liquid.

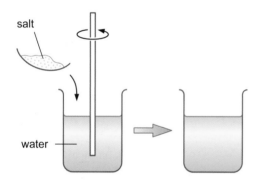

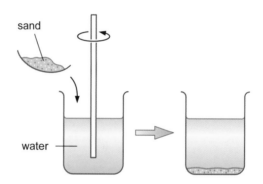

The salt dissolves in the water but the sand doesn't.

When the salt dissolves in the water it makes a **solution**.

You can still see the sand, but the salt seems to have vanished.

- The salt is called the **solute** – it is the solid that dissolves.
- The water is called the **solvent** – it is the liquid that dissolves the solid.

The salt dissolves in water. We say that salt is soluble in water.

Sand does not dissolve in water. We say that sand is insoluble in water.

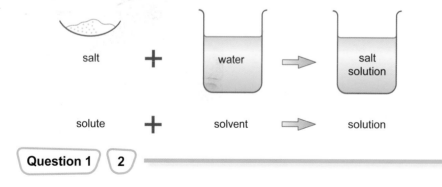

Question 1 ⟩ 2 ⟩

Everyday mixtures

The word 'pure' on a bottle of mineral water means that nothing has been added to the water. However, this 'pure' mineral water contains a lot of different minerals dissolved in water and is really a mixture. The label has a list of substances dissolved in the water a bit like the one shown. When you see 'mg/litre', it means 'thousandths of a gram in a litre'.

In science, the word 'pure' means something that contains only a single substance and not a mixture of substances. A scientist would not describe mineral water as 'pure'.

Mixtures are found everywhere.

- Mineral water is a mixture of water and dissolved minerals.
- Coffee is a mixture of water and coffee. Some people add milk or sugar when they drink it.
- Milk is mainly a mixture of water, sugar, protein and fat.
- Sea water is mainly a mixture of water and dissolved salt.

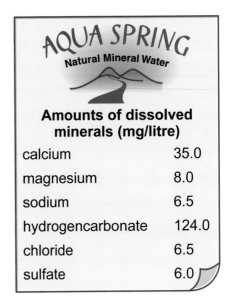

AQUA SPRING
Natural Mineral Water

Amounts of dissolved minerals (mg/litre)

calcium	35.0
magnesium	8.0
sodium	6.5
hydrogencarbonate	124.0
chloride	6.5
sulfate	6.0

 Question 3 **4**

Separating a mixture of sand and water

The sand is insoluble. It does not dissolve in the water. The sand can be separated from the water using a method called **filtration**.

The sand and water mixture is poured through a filter paper. The filter paper acts like a very fine sieve.

The water goes through the paper. Water particles are much smaller than the holes in the paper. The sand is trapped on the paper. Sand particles are much larger than the holes in the paper.

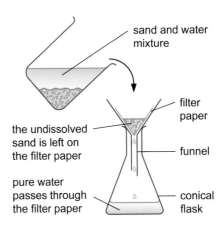

sand and water mixture

the undissolved sand is left on the filter paper

filter paper

funnel

pure water passes through the filter paper

conical flask

Separating sand and water.

Question 5

Separating a mixture of salt and water

Salt water is a mixture of salt and water. The salt is soluble, so it dissolves in the water. It is called a solution of salt in water. The salt particles are now a similar size to the water particles. Filtering does not work. The salt solution just goes straight through the filter paper. All the particles are smaller than the holes in the paper. The salt is separated from the water by a method called **evaporation**.

When you heat the salt solution, the water evaporates into the air. The salt does not evaporate and is left behind on the evaporating dish.

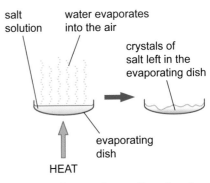

salt solution

water evaporates into the air

crystals of salt left in the evaporating dish

HEAT

evaporating dish

Separating salt and water.

Question 6

You should already know | Outcomes | Keywords

The chemical name for salt is **sodium chloride**. Sodium chloride is often called 'common salt'. There are two main places where we find salt.

- Some types of rock contain a lot of salt. This is called rock salt.
- Sea water contains a lot of salt.

Getting salt out of rock or sea water is important all over the world.

Crushed rock salt.

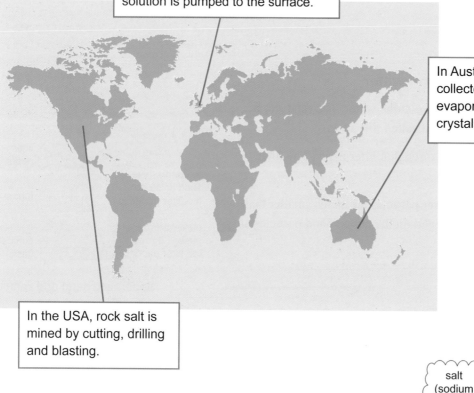

In the UK, water is pumped into the rock salt. The salt dissolves and salt solution is pumped to the surface.

In Australia, sea water is collected. Sunlight is used to evaporate the water until salt crystals form.

In the USA, rock salt is mined by cutting, drilling and blasting.

Salt and rock salt have a lot of uses.

Rock salt is crushed and spread on roads in winter. The salt melts snow or ice and makes driving conditions a lot safer.

Three important chemicals that are made from salt are chlorine, sodium carbonate and sodium hydroxide.

chlorine
used to make bleach

sodium carbonate
used to make glass

salt (sodium chloride)

rock salt
spread on roads in winter to melt snow and ice

sodium hydroxide
used to make soap and detergents

Some uses of salt.

Question 1 / 2

What happens when salt dissolves?

When you dissolve salt in water, you get a clear colourless solution. The salt seems to vanish.

Before the salt dissolves, it is a solid. The particles it is made of are held together in groups that are big enough to see as salt crystals.

When the salt crystals dissolve, they break up into the tiny particles that make them. These particles mix in amongst the water particles. If you evaporate the water, you get salt crystals back.

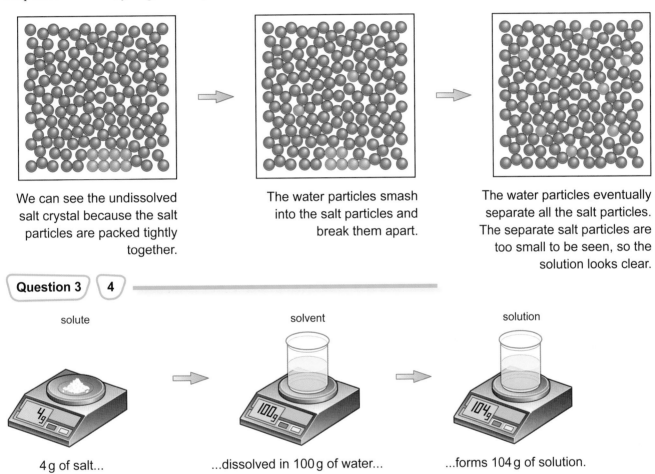

We can see the undissolved salt crystal because the salt particles are packed tightly together.

The water particles smash into the salt particles and break them apart.

The water particles eventually separate all the salt particles. The separate salt particles are too small to be seen, so the solution looks clear.

Question 3 **4**

solute

solvent

solution

4 g of salt...

...dissolved in 100 g of water...

...forms 104 g of solution.

You can show that the salt particles are still in the water when they dissolve by using a balance.

The mass of a solution equals the total mass of the solute and the solvent. This is true for any solution. We can write this as an equation:

mass of solute + mass of solvent = mass of solution

When a solute dissolves, it hasn't really vanished. It is part of the solution. No mass is lost. This is called **conservation of mass**.

Question 5 **6**

Getting the solvent back from a solution

Bathroom mirrors steam up when you have a hot bath. The hot steam from the bath hits the cold mirror. The cold mirror cools the steam back into water. This is called **condensation**.

The idea that steam changes back into water when the steam hits a cold surface can help us get the water back from a salt solution.

When a salt solution is heated up, the water **evaporates** as steam. This means that the water changes state from a liquid to a gas. The steam can be condensed back into pure water by cooling it down. The steam changes state from a gas back into a liquid when it hits a cold surface.

Everyday condensation.

Question 1

If you want to collect the water that is formed when the steam condenses, you need a special bit of apparatus to do that. The water is collected using a **condenser**.

This whole process is called **distillation**. During distillation the solute doesn't evaporate The solute is left behind in the flask. The pure water made by distillation is called distilled water.

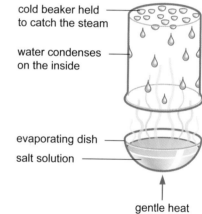

cold beaker held to catch the steam

water condenses on the inside

evaporating dish

salt solution

gentle heat

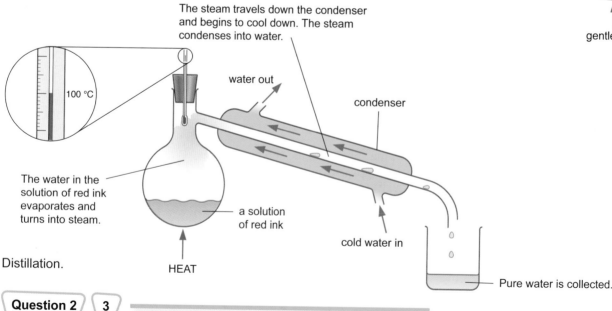

The steam travels down the condenser and begins to cool down. The steam condenses into water.

100 °C

water out

condenser

The water in the solution of red ink evaporates and turns into steam.

a solution of red ink

cold water in

Pure water is collected.

Distillation.

HEAT

Question 2 3

Chromatography

Some solutions contain a mixture of different solutes. We separate a mixture of two or more solutes using **chromatography**.

This diagram shows one method used to do chromatography.

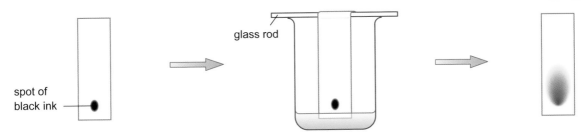

A spot of black ink is placed on the chromatography paper.

The paper is suspended in the water. The spot of ink must be above the level of the water.

The black ink separates into different colours. Each colour is a different solute in the original ink mixture.

The piece of paper you get at the end of doing chromatography is called a **chromatogram**.

The water dissolves the ink. As the water soaks up the paper, it carries the ink particles with it. Different ink particles are carried different distances before they get left behind on the paper. You can see the different solutes on the chromatogram.

Question 4

Using chromatography

You can use chromatography to study the dyes used in food.
The chromatogram shows that the blue and yellow food colourings are pure substances. They only contain one substance.

The brown food colouring is a mixture of the yellow and blue colourings with a third colour mixed in.

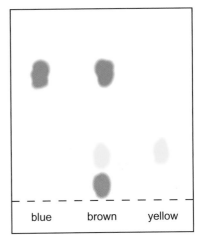

Chromatography results for blue, brown and yellow food colourings.

Question 5

Scientists use chromatography to help them in a wide range of situations. These include:

- finding out which pigments are contained in leaves;
- comparing the blood of a suspect with blood found at the scene of a crime;
- testing urine to check a patient's health.

A chromatogram of urine from a healthy person.

A chromatogram of urine from a patient suffering from phenylketonuria.

Question 6

Check your progress

If we keep adding salt to water at room temperature, there comes a point when no more salt will dissolve. A solution in which no more solid will dissolve is called a **saturated solution**.

Some solids will dissolve in water. We say they are **soluble** in water. Others will not, and we say they are **insoluble** in water. Some solids are soluble in different amounts. For example, sodium chloride dissolves easily in water but lead chloride is quite hard to dissolve in water. We say it is only slightly soluble.

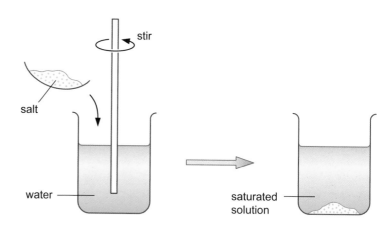

Making a saturated solution of salt in water.

Solubility is a measure of how much solute will dissolve in a solvent. The higher its solubility, the more solute will dissolve.

To compare the solubilities of different solutes, you measure the maximum mass of a solute that will dissolve in 100 g of the solvent. You are measuring how much solute makes a saturated solution in 100 g of water.

Substance	Solubility in grams in 100 g of water at 20 °C
calcium chloride	74
copper sulfate	21
potassium chlorate	7
potassium nitrate	300
sand	0
sodium chloride	36

To dissolve a solid. you need to use a solvent that will work. Water does not dissolve everything. For example, some types of ink are soluble in alcohol but not in water.

This means that you must name the solvent when you state solubility. For example, in the table, the column heading states 'Solubility in grams in 100 g of water at 20 °C'.

Question 1 2 3

Temperature and solubility

Sugar is easy to dissolve in a cup of hot tea. It is not so easy to dissolve if the tea is cold.

The solubility of most solutes increases when the temperature goes up. More solute dissolves in a warm solvent than in a cold solvent. This means that it is important that you give the temperature when you state the solubility. For example, sodium chloride has a solubility of 36 g in 100 g of water <u>at 20 °C</u>.

A good way of showing how solubility has different values at different temperatures is to use a graph. You plot the temperature along the bottom axis and the solubility up the side. The graph shows the solubilities for lead nitrate, copper sulfate and potassium chloride.

This graph shows that the solubilities of all three solids increase when the temperature goes up.

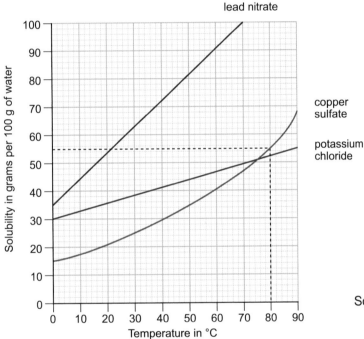

Solubility curves for three solids.

The curves can be used to work out the solubility of any of the solids at any temperature. For example, the dotted line going up from 80 °C shows that the solubility of copper sulfate in 100 g of water at 80 °C is 55 g.

You can also see that the lines for potassium chloride and copper sulfate cross at 75 °C. This means that they have the same solubility at that temperature.

You can also see that, for all the temperatures shown on the graph, the solubility of lead nitrate is higher than those of copper sulfate and potassium chloride.

Review your work

Question 4   5   6

Summary ➡

You should already know

Outcomes

Keywords

Dissolving salt in water

A group of pupils are discussing how to investigate how temperature affects how much salt will dissolve in water. They are trying to think of the different things that might affect the result. These are called **variables**.

The volume of water matters.

Yes, we need to keep it the same for a fair test.

Salt dissolves faster in hot water than it does in cold.

We can measure the amount of salt by the number of spatulas we add.

Question 1 2

The pupils decide to count the number of spatulas of salt that will dissolve in 50 cm³ of water. They will count how many spatulas of salt they can add until no more dissolves. They will repeat the experiment at a different temperatures from 20 °C to 90 °C.

This means that the variable they will change is the water temperature.

They will count the number of spatulas that will dissolve. This is the variable that depends on the water temperature.

The volume of water is a variable that is being kept the same so the test is fair.

The variable you change is called the **independent variable**, or sometimes the input variable. The variable you measure as the result is called the **dependent variable** or the output variable.

The variables you keep the same are called **control variables**.

Question 3 4 5

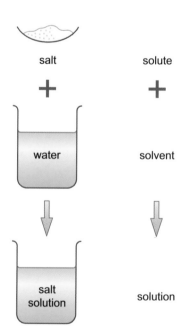

salt   solute

+   +

water   solvent

salt solution   solution

In the experiment, salt will be added to water to make salt solution.

Rules for plotting a graph

Put the independent variable on the bottom axis.

Put the dependent variable on the side axis.

Label the axes and put in any units (such as °C).

Use fine crosses to mark points.

Analysing results

The students produce a table of results like this.

Temperature of water (°C)	22	31	39	50	61
Number of spatulas of salt	5	6	7	9	12

The results table is good because it has clear headings with units.

The rules for showing the results on a graph are given in the box.

They produce a graph like this one.

It has three mistakes on it before they draw the line!

One of them is that they should have put the temperature on the bottom axis because it is the independent variable.

The number of spatulas is the output of the experiment. This is the dependent variable and it goes on the side axis not along the bottom.

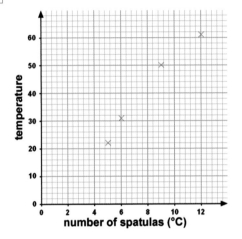

 Question 6 **7**

Here are the results and the graph for another experiment, to find out how much salt you can get out of rock salt. The graph is shown before the line is drawn and it already has three mistakes. See if you can spot them.

Mass of rock salt (g)	5	10	15	20	25
Mass of salt extracted (g)	1	3	6	8	10

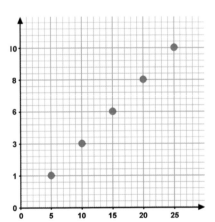

 Question 8 **9**

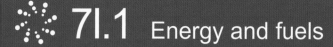

| You should already know | Outcomes | Keywords |

Energy is an important idea in science. We measure energy in **joules**. Energy is found in different situations, called 'forms' or 'types'.

Gravitational potential energy is stored in things that are high up.

Fuels store **chemical energy**.

A moving object has **kinetic energy**.

Heat energy is given out by hot objects.

Sound energy is given out by loudspeakers.

Light energy is given out by luminous objects.

Elastic potential energy is stored in things that are squashed or stretched.

Electrical energy is the energy carried by electricity.

We need energy to make things happen.

The rocket needs energy to take off.

The microwave oven needs energy to cook.

The cheetah needs energy to run.

The plant needs energy to grow.

Question 1   2

When something happens, energy <u>transfers</u> from one type to another.

The picture shows one example of a transfer.

Sometimes, when something happens, the energy transfers into more than one type.

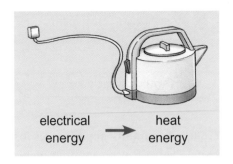

electrical energy → heat energy

What happens	Energy transfer
something burning, like coal or wood	<u>chemical</u> energy transfers to <u>heat</u> energy and <u>light</u> energy
an electric fire heating a room	<u>electrical</u> energy transfers to <u>heat</u> energy and <u>light</u> energy
a car speeding up	<u>chemical</u> energy transfers to <u>kinetic</u> energy, <u>sound</u> energy and <u>heat</u> energy

Some examples of energy transfer.

Question 3 **4**

Useful fuels

Fuels have chemical energy stored in them. When we burn a fuel, the chemical energy transfers to heat.

- In a power station, heat is transferred to electrical energy by generators.
- A Bunsen burner burns methane to produce heat energy.
- Petrol burns inside a car engine to produce movement.
- Wax burns in a candle to produce light energy.

We burn fuels to do jobs for us. These jobs usually fit into one of four categories: transport, heating, cooking and making electricity.

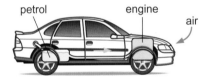

Fuels won't burn without oxygen from the air.

Oil is used to heat schools.

Gas is used to cook.

Coal is used to generate electricity.

Aircraft use aviation fuel.

Question 5 **6**

You should already know | Outcomes | Keywords

Coal, oil and natural gas are all fossil fuels. We burn them to use them as fuels. They are also useful for making materials like plastics.

You can see the fossilised remains of plants in coal.

This is because coal is made from the remains of trees and other plants that died millions of years ago.

The plants stored energy from the sunlight as they grew. When the plants died they were buried under layers of mud. The buried plants gradually turned into coal over millions of years.

The diagrams show how coal was formed from trees and how oil and gas were formed from the remains of sea creatures.

This piece of coal has the fossilised remains of a plant in it.

Trees store energy from sunlight as they grow.

Dead trees fall into swamps.

The dead trees are buried under layers of mud.

The wood gradually turns into coal.

How coal was formed.

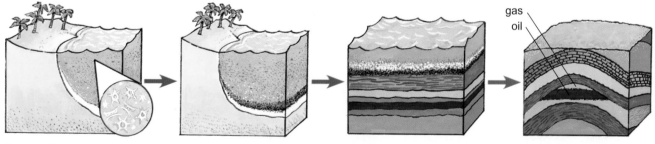

Sea creatures store energy.

These creatures die and sink to the bottom.

The dead creatures are buried under layers of sand.

gas
oil

The creatures gradually turn into oil and gas which are trapped under rock.

How oil and gas were formed.

Fossil fuels will run out

All the fossil fuels take many millions of years to form. We are using them up very quickly. They are not being replaced. Fossil fuels are non-renewable. This means that one day they will run out.

Question 1 | 2 | 3

We use fossil fuels to make most of our electricity

People started to use electrical energy from the end of the 19th century. Thomas Edison invented the electric light bulb in 1879. Since then, we have used electricity more and more. At the start of the 21st century, most people would find it almost impossible to live without electrical energy.

Most of our electrical energy comes from the chemical energy in fossil fuels.

Fossil fuel	Advantages	Disadvantages
coal	• reliable • plentiful supply	• needs to be transported and stored • burning it contributes to acid rain and global warming
oil	• can transport it in pipes	• needs to be transported and stored • bad sea pollution possible from oil spills from tankers • burning it contributes to acid rain and global warming
natural gas	• burns more cleanly than others	• difficult to drill for • needs to be transported and stored • burning it contributes to acid rain and global warming

fuel oil

coal

North Sea gas

Power stations mainly burn these fuels.

It is important to find alternatives to fossil fuels

It is important to save fossil fuels because they are running out. They also have important uses as raw materials to make plastics. Burning them is the main cause of global warming, acid rain and pollution.

Fossil fuels can be saved by:

• using other sources of energy to make electricity;
• using devices that need less energy to do the same job, like energy efficient light bulbs.

One alternative to using fossil fuels is nuclear power. This uses the heat from radioactive substances to produce electricity. This is done using a nuclear reactor. Nuclear reactors produce radiation, which is dangerous. Thick concrete walls are built around them to protect us. One advantage of using nuclear power stations is that they do not give off gases that cause global warming or acid rain, but there is always a risk to the environment if there is an accident.

It is also important to remember that the processes of building the nuclear power station and manufacturing the fuel for it both contribute to global warming.

Gases from car exhausts cause air pollution.

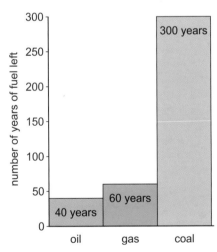

number of years of fuel left

oil — 40 years
gas — 60 years
coal — 300 years

Bar chart showing when fossil fuels will run out, based on current rates of consumption of known world reserves.

Question 4　5　6

Check your progress

Fossil fuels will run out one day. We say they are non-renewable resources. They also cause pollution and global warming. We need alternative sources of energy. These are called **renewable** energy resources because they will never run out.

Energy resources such as **wind** energy and **wave** energy will last as long as the Sun keeps shining. They do not get used up like coal or oil.

Many renewable energy resources get their energy from the Sun. The wind, a wave on the sea and **hydro-electric** power stations all get their energy from the Sun.

The Sun will keep on shining for about 5 billion more years.

So solar energy is a renewable energy resource.

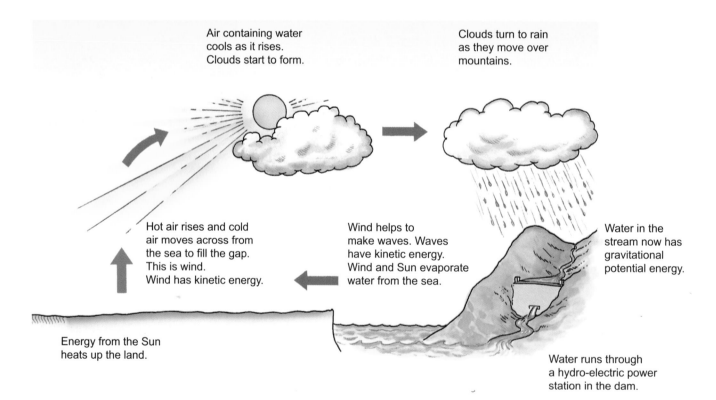

Air containing water cools as it rises. Clouds start to form.

Clouds turn to rain as they move over mountains.

Hot air rises and cold air moves across from the sea to fill the gap. This is wind. Wind has kinetic energy.

Wind helps to make waves. Waves have kinetic energy. Wind and Sun evaporate water from the sea.

Water in the stream now has gravitational potential energy.

Energy from the Sun heats up the land.

Water runs through a hydro-electric power station in the dam.

Not all renewable energy resources depend on the Sun. Energy from **tides** comes from the gravitational pull of the Moon.

Geothermal energy comes from the heat energy in hot rocks deep underground.

Question 1   2   3

Biomass energy

Plants need energy from the Sun to grow. This energy is stored in all the material from which the plant is made. This includes material like the wood from trees. The energy stored in plant material is known as **biomass** energy. You can burn plant material, or use some plants like sugar cane to make a liquid fuel that can be used in cars. Provided you do not use the plant material up faster than it can be grown, biomass is renewable.

Energy is transferred to trees by sunlight. Trees store this energy as they grow. So trees are stores of chemical energy. You can burn the wood as a fuel.

Solar energy

You can use solar cells to transfer the Sun's energy directly into electricity. This is used in garden lights and pocket calculators. Many satellites use solar energy as their power source. It is expensive to use solar cells to produce large amounts of electricity because you need a huge area of cells. Solar cells do not work at night.

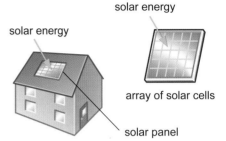

solar energy

solar energy

array of solar cells

solar panel

Wind energy

The kinetic energy of the wind is used to turn a turbine. This drives a generator to make electricity. Wind turbines are being used in more and more places. Some people object to the appearance of wind turbines and they only produce electricity when the wind blows.

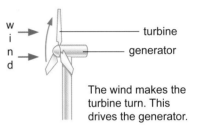

wind

turbine

generator

The wind makes the turbine turn. This drives the generator.

Tidal energy

This energy comes from the gravitational pull of the Moon. A barrier is built across the mouth of a river. The water is trapped behind the barrier at high tide. At low tide, the water flows back through turbines in the barrier. The turbines drive generators to produce electricity. This source of energy does not produce any pollution but the building costs are very high.

When the barrage is full, the mud flats in the estuary are flooded all the time.

Wave energy

The waves on the sea get their energy from the winds, which are driven by the Sun. There are several ways of getting the energy from waves. One way is to use the up-and-down movement of the water to push air past a turbine. The turbine drives a generator to make electricity.

This source of energy does not cause any pollution. It is not yet used commercially. The disadvantage is that the machinery used can be corroded by the salty sea water.

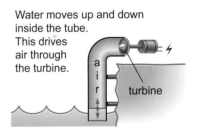

Water moves up and down inside the tube. This drives air through the turbine.

air

turbine

Geothermal energy

The rocks deep underground are hot from the heat produced in the Earth's core. You can pump water down into sections of rock that are cracked and the water will return to the surface as steam. The heat energy in the steam can be used to drive turbines to make electricity.

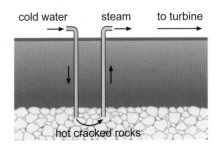

cold water   steam   to turbine

hot cracked rocks

Question 4 5 6 7

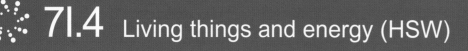
You should already know | Outcomes | Keywords

We need energy from food for everything we do

All living things, including us, use energy. All activity, including just being alive, needs energy. Food is the energy resource that animals and plants need to live and to do things.

Different activities need different amounts of energy. A small apple has a mass of about 100 g. To lift a small apple up by 1 m needs about 1 **joule** of energy.

A joule isn't a very large measure of energy. Sometimes the **kilojoule** is used instead. 1 kilojoule is 1000 joules. The pictures show how any kilojoules are needed for different activities.

Jogging needs 60 kilojoules of energy for every minute you jog.

Riding a bike needs 30 kilojoules of energy for every minute you ride.

Walking needs 20 kilojoules of energy for every minute you stroll along.

Sleeping needs 6 kilojoules of energy for every minute you sleep.

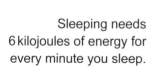

Question 1 / 2 / 3

Animals eat food to get their energy

Animals need to eat food to get energy. Food labels show how much chemical energy is stored in the food. As well as using kilojoules, the labels sometimes use an old unit for energy called the kilocalorie (kcal).

This is just same as having different units for length, like centimetres and inches. You can use either of the units to tells you how much chemical energy is stored in food.

Food A

NUTRITION INFORMATION
100 g provides: Energy 1500 kJ / 370 kcal. Protein 4.5 g. Carbohydrate 67 g. (of which sugars 29 g) (starch 33 g). Fat 10 g (of which saturates 2 g). Fibre 3 g. Sodium 0.3 g. Vitamins: Thiamin B_1 1 mg (70%). Riboflavin B_2 1.1 mg (70%). Niacin 12 mg (70%). Vitamin B_6 1.4 mg (70%). Folic Acid 135 µg (70%). Vitamin B_{12} 0.7 µg (70%). Minerals: Calcium 540 mg (70%). Iron 6.4 mg (45%).

Food B

NUTRITION INFORMATION	PER PIECE	PER 100 g
ENERGY:	1180 kJ / 281 kcal	1885 kJ / 449 kcal
PROTEIN:	2.6 g	4.2 g
CARBOHYDRATE:	43.1 g	69.0 g
FAT:	10.9 g	17.4 g

Nutrition labels.

Question 4

When people go on diets, they sometimes 'count the calories' in the food they eat. This is a way of estimating how much energy their body is getting from food based on the old measuring unit. If you use less energy in activities than you get from your food then you put on weight. If you use more energy than you get from your food then you lose weight. That is why exercise helps to keep weight down and why people in active jobs need more food than people who sit at a desk all day.

The energy stored in food is calculated very carefully for extreme situations like space travel, polar exploration and long-distance yacht racing. In these situations, it is important to use foods that provide a lot of energy but only take up a little space.

Question 5

The energy in food comes from the Sun

Like all living things, plants need food to live and grow. Plants make their own food using the energy in sunlight. Animals get their energy from plants or other animals.

Patrick eats meat, which comes from an animal. The animal he eats got its energy from plants in the first place. The plants got their energy to live and grow from the Sun. This means that all our food energy resources originally came from the Sun.

This potato plant used the energy in sunlight to make its food.

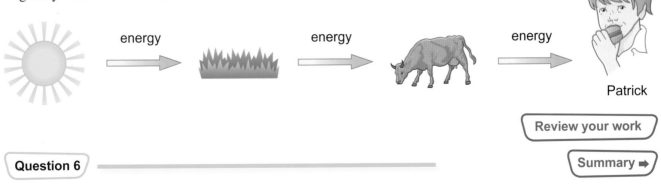

energy   energy   energy

Patrick

Review your work

Question 6

Summary ➡

You should already know

Outcomes

Keywords

What are ethical and moral implications?

Some people think that building a wind farm is a good thing because it supplies renewable energy and does not pollute the atmosphere when it is operating. Other people object because it changes the appearance of the landscape. This is referred to as visual pollution. Wind turbines also create some noise pollution when they operate.

Deciding whether or not to build a wind farm will be a decision based on many things, some for and some against.

Considering the **ethical** and **moral** implications means thinking about the positive and negative impact of the decision on the lives of people, plants, animals and the environment in general.

Worn out wind turbines will be relatively cheap to dismantle. They don't contain dangerous materials. Wind farms don't pollute the air with waste gases. But some people object to their appearance and the noise they make. They might be prepared to pay more for electricity to avoid having generators in beauty spots.

Meeting the demand for energy

Our demand for energy is very high. The fossil fuels we have been using for the past two hundred years or so are running out. Using them causes pollution and global warming. Finding alternatives to diesel and petrol for road transport would help considerably. One idea being studied is to use hydrogen as a fuel.

- Solar cells produce electricity.
- The electricity is used to get the hydrogen out of water, and this is stored in a tank.
- Your car is converted to use hydrogen gas as a fuel.

The advantage of burning hydrogen in a car rather than petrol is that the waste product is water and there is no pollution.

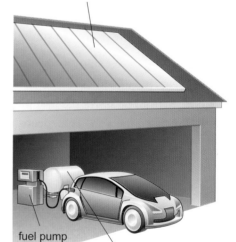

combined solar cell and electrolyser – produces hydrogen

fuel pump

storage cylinder for compressed hydrogen gas

A scheme for powering hydrogen-fuelled cars from sunlight.

Question 1 2

Problems to solve

Alternatives to fossil fuels have advantages but there are also concerns about them and problems to solve. Some of these problems are **technical**. Some are ethical and moral.

Problem	Possible solution
You need six hundred of the most powerful wind turbines operating all the time to produce as much electricity as one coal fired power station.	Make a better design of wind turbine that produces more electricity.
Hydro-electricity does not cause pollution but there are very few hydro-electric sites in the UK.	Flood more areas of land to construct hydro-electric schemes.
Nuclear power stations don't pollute the air but they produce radioactive waste that will be dangerous for thousands of years.	Seal the waste in concrete blocks that will keep it safe for a few hundred years and hope that future generations find a way of dealing with it.

Question 3 4 5

One thing leads to another

In science, a development can produce a new problem that was not expected. An example is the use of power lines.

However we produce electricity, we need to transport it across the country using power lines. In recent years, this has led to concerns about people becoming ill. This was not expected when power lines were built.

Power lines give off signals a bit similar to radio signals. In a few small areas, there have been reports of a higher level of a fatal illness called leukaemia (cancer of the blood) in people who live near power lines.

There is no definite evidence that living near power lines is dangerous. There are teams of scientists trying to answer this question. If they find that there is a problem then the solution will be either to move the cables or to move the people. In either case, it will have a big effect on the way people live.

Similar concerns have been expressed about mobile phones and mobile phone masts. The use of mobile phones has had a big impact on the way people live. If we find out there is a danger then the solution to the problem will probably produce another big change in the way people live.

Question 6

Hydro-electric dams do not pollute but they need a large area of flooded land.

The waste from nuclear power stations is very dangerous for thousands of years.

Power lines give out very low frequency, very long wavelength signals.

Zap your brain with a mobile phone!

It's good to talk.

7J.1 Switches, circuits and symbols

Making a circuit

Electricity will only flow when there is a complete path to conduct the electricity. We call this a complete **circuit**. These diagrams show four attempts at making a **bulb** light up. Only one will work.

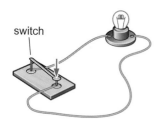

There is no source of energy to make the electricity flow, so the bulb will not light up.

There is a gap. It is not a complete circuit, so the electricity cannot flow around.

This circuit is connected using wood. Wood does not let electricity flow through it. Wood is not a conductor.

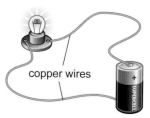

This is a complete circuit. Electricity can flow and the bulb will light up.

Using a switch

Sometimes we need to be able to break the circuit to stop the electricity flowing. We can do this by using a **switch**. When a switch is closed, the circuit is complete and electricity can flow. When the switch is open, the circuit is not complete and so electricity cannot flow.

A torch is a device that contains a simple circuit. A battery is connected to a switch and a bulb. When the torch is needed the switch can be closed. This makes a complete circuit and the bulb lights up.

When the torch is not being used, the switch is opened. This breaks the complete circuit and the bulb goes out. This stops the battery running down.

You can break the circuit with a switch. No electricity then flows.

When the circuit is complete, electricity flows through the switch and the bulb.

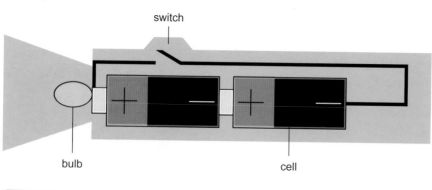

Question 1 2

Drawing a circuit

It is useful to have an easy way of drawing the components in a circuit. Instead of drawing pictures, we use symbols to represent the components.

There are many different symbols for components in circuits.

The **circuit diagram** shows two cells connected together in a complete circuit with a bulb. The arrows on the connection lines show the flow of the electric current.

When you connect two or more cells together, you make a battery. The symbol in the table for a battery can be used when you do not know how many cells there are. The symbol in the circuit diagram shows a battery made from two cells.

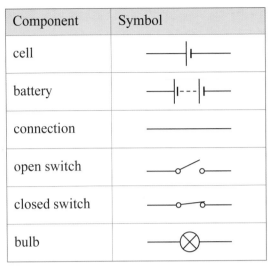

Component	Symbol
cell	
battery	
connection	
open switch	
closed switch	
bulb	

Six common symbols.

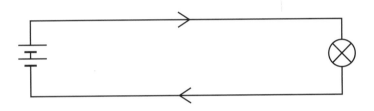

Question 3 **4**

Where do the symbols for a cell and a battery come from?

In 1780, an Italian scientist called Luigi Galvani was studying frogs' legs. He put the legs from a dead frog on a copper hook attached to an iron wire. The legs twitched even though they were dead. Galvani thought electricity must be producing electrical pulses in the nerves to make the muscles move.

Another Italian scientist called Alessandro Volta guessed that the electricity was coming from a reaction between the copper, iron and the salt water used to preserve the legs. Volta experimented with combinations of different metals like copper, zinc, silver and iron to make a pile of plates that produced electricity.

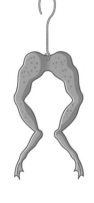

The diagram shows a pile made out of silver discs and zinc discs separated by cardboard pads soaked in salt water. A single cell is made from one silver disc and one zinc disc separated by a cardboard disc. The whole pile of cells is called a battery. Volta's pile was the first battery ever made. The symbols for a cell and a battery include lines to represent the plates in Volta's pile.

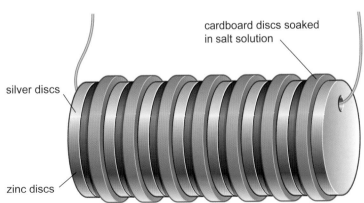

cardboard discs soaked in salt solution

silver discs

zinc discs

Question 5 **6**

You should already know | Outcomes | Keywords

The things in an electric circuit like bulbs and batteries are called **components**.

In a **series** circuit, all the components are connected in one loop. This diagram shows a circuit with two bulbs in series.

There is only one path around the circuit for the **current** to follow. All of the current has to flow through each of the components in the circuit.

We say that this current flows from the positive side of the **power supply**, around the circuit and back to the negative side of the power supply.

This direction of flow is shown by arrowheads on the diagram.

We measure the size of an electric current using an **ammeter**. An ammeter shows the value of the current in **amperes** (amps or 'A' for short).

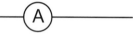 This is the symbol for an ammeter.

The ammeter is connected in the circuit so that the electric current flows through the meter. It is put in series with the other components.

The diagram shows how it should be connected.

The ammeter in the diagram is showing a reading of 0.15 amps, which is written as 0.15 A.

The diagrams below show the places where an ammeter can be put in a series circuit.

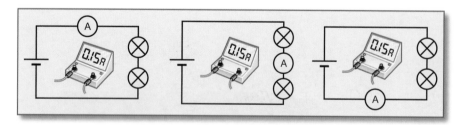

All of the ammeters show the same reading, which shows that the electric current stays the same all the way round a series circuit. The current does not get used up. It stays the same as it passes through each bulb.

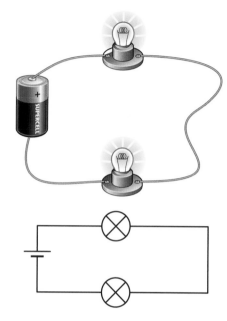

Two bulbs in a series circuit.

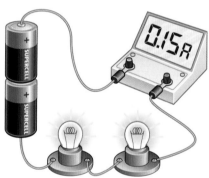

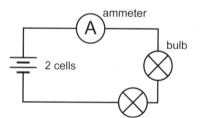

ammeter
bulb
2 cells

Question 1 2 3

Changing the current

Dimmer switches can be used to change the brightness of lights.
The circuits show three different dimmer switch settings and how
these affect the size of the current and the brightness of the bulbs.

It is harder for the current to flow through some materials. We say that
these materials have a high **resistance**. The current gets smaller if the
resistance of a circuit is increased.

Resistors are components that have a known amount of resistance.

Variable resistors have a resistance that can be changed, often by turning a
knob. Volume and tone controls are usually made from variable resistors.

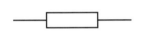

This is the symbol for a resistor.

This is the symbol for a variable resistor.

Turn up the volume control.

If you make the resistance larger then the current will be smaller, provided
you do not change anything else.

A dimmer switch is an example of a variable resistor. As you turn the
dimmer switch, you change the resistance. Increasing the resistance
decreases the current and makes the bulb dimmer. Decreasing the
resistance increases the current and makes the bulb brighter.

All electrical components have their own resistance. Changing the number
of bulbs in a circuit changes the total resistance of that circuit.

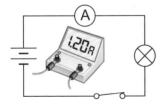 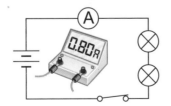 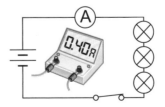

As bulbs are added to this circuit, the total resistance increases. This means
the current decreases if you keep the same number of cells in the circuit.
The bulbs become less bright as the current falls.

Question 4 5 6

You should already know | Outcomes | Keywords

A source of energy is needed for a current to flow around a circuit.

The **cell** or **battery** provides the energy to make the current flow.

Cells and batteries

This picture shows a torch. The energy to make this torch light up is supplied by two cells. Two or more cells connected together are called a battery. In science, the word 'battery' means ' a group of cells'. Unfortunately, in everyday English, the word 'battery' is also used to refer to a single cell. This can be very confusing.

Cells and batteries have a number marked on them with a letter V after it. This is the number of volts for the cell or battery. It tells us how strong the cell or battery is.

A higher voltage can mean brighter bulbs, but you have to be careful. A voltage that is too high will blow the bulb and it will stop working.

The most common cell used in everyday appliances is a 1.5 V cell. Some appliances use a 9 V battery with two studs on top. The 9 V battery in the diagram is actually made of six tiny 1.5 V cells in a stack inside the case. It actually is a battery in the scientific sense of the word.

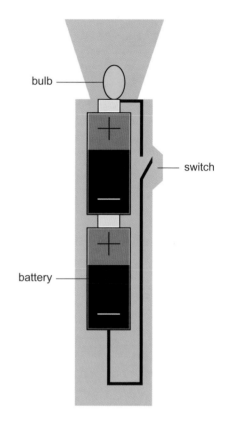
bulb — switch — battery

A 1.5 V cell.

Two 1.5 V cells make a 3.0 V battery.

Three 1.5 V cells make a 4.5 V battery.

A 9 V battery has six cells hidden inside the case.

Question 1 / 2

Inside a cell

When a cell is connected in a complete circuit, it makes the current flow. Inside the cell are chemicals that react together. It is this chemical reaction that makes the current flow.

When you connect cells together to make a battery, you need to make sure that the positive end of one cell is connected to the negative end of the next.

The most common type of cell produces a voltage of 1.5 volts. There are several different ways of making this type of cell. The diagram shows one very common way of making a cell, known as a 'zinc–carbon' cell.

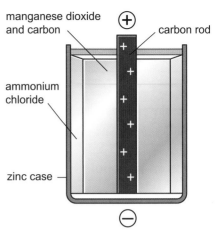

Cross-section of a zinc–carbon cell.

Question 3

Inside a circuit

It can be difficult to picture what happens in an electric circuit because you can't see anything moving. The flow of electric current around a circuit can be compared to the flow of water around a system of pipes.

The cell or battery is like the pump.

If you put an ammeter in the electrical circuit, it would be like putting a paddle wheel in the water circuit to show how fast the water is flowing. The ammeter measures the flow of an electric current in amperes.

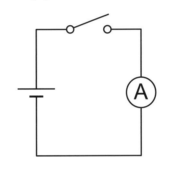
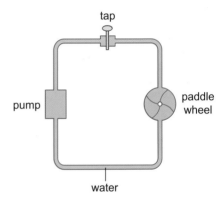

Electric current		Water current	
Object	Job	Object	Job
battery	pushes the current around the circuit	pump	pushes the water around the pipes
current	flows around the circuit	water	flows around the pipes
ammeter	shows how fast the current flows around the circuit	paddle wheel	shows how fast the water flows around the pipes
switch	breaks the circuit and the flow of current	tap	stops the flow of water

Comparing an electrical circuit to a water circuit.

Question 4

So far, the circuits we have studied have been series circuits. The other main type of circuit is called a **parallel** circuit.

Bulbs in parallel

In a series circuit, there is just one route for the current around the circuit. In parallel circuits, there are junctions where the current can go along two or more different routes.

This circuit diagram shows two bulbs connected in parallel. The electric current leaves the battery. When it gets to junction A, some of the current goes through bulb 1 and some through bulb 2. The current splits up.

When the current reaches junction B, it joins back together again and travels back to the battery.

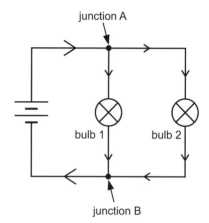

Electric current in parallel circuits

In a parallel circuit, the total current from the battery is the same as the current through each of the separate branches added together.

This diagram shows two identical bulbs connected in parallel; these bulbs have the same resistance. The electric current flowing through each bulb is the same, 0.5 A.

The current from the battery is the same as the current through the bulbs added together:

0.5 A + 0.5 A = 1.0 A

In this diagram, the three bulbs are identical. This means the current in bulb C must be the same as the current in the other bulbs, 2 A.

If each bulb has a current of 2 A then the current flowing at point X must be 6 A. This is because the current from the battery is the same as the current through the bulbs added together.

The same current goes back into the battery as leaves it, so the current at point Y is also 6 A.

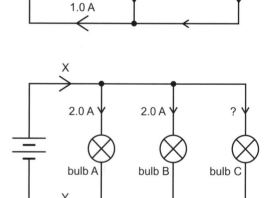

Question 1 2 3

Bright bulbs in parallel

In a parallel circuit, each bulb is connected directly to the battery. The voltage across each bulb is the same as the voltage across the battery. This means that all of the bulbs are bright. When you connect more bulbs in parallel, the current from the battery increases. If you have a lot of bulbs connected, the battery will go flat very quickly!

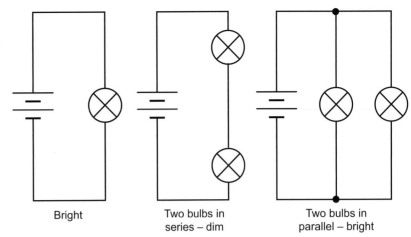

Bright   Two bulbs in   Two bulbs in
                series – dim   parallel – bright

Question 4

Series or parallel?

When designing an electrical circuit, you need to consider whether a series or a parallel circuit is the best.

Some Christmas tree lights are wired in series. The lights in houses are wired in parallel.

The parallel circuit is better if you want to be able to switch each light on or off on its own. This is what you want for the lights in a house. The series circuit can be safer because the current in the circuit is smaller and you do not need as much wire to connect the bulbs. A series circuit can be useful if you want to light several bulbs that do not need to be very bright.

The series circuit is also good for Christmas tree lights because, if you can get special bulbs that flash on and off, you only need one of them in a series circuit and it makes <u>all</u> the bulbs flash on and off.

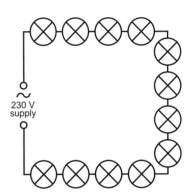

Tree lights in series

Series circuit	Parallel circuit
if one bulb blows, all the bulbs go out	if one bulb blows, it does not affect the others
one switch operates all of the bulbs	each bulb can be turned on or off with its own switch
the power supply voltage is shared between the bulbs	each bulb gets the full power supply voltage
the current from the power supply is low	the current from the power supply is high

A comparison between series and parallel circuits.

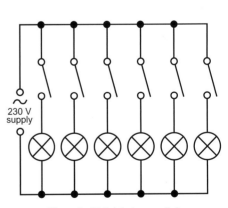

Household lights in parallel

Question 5 **6** **7**

Check your progress

You should already know   Outcomes   Keywords

Electricity is very useful but it can also be very dangerous. We need to protect ourselves when using electricity, especially when it is **mains electricity**. This uses a higher voltage than batteries.

Safety at home

Most accidents with electricity are caused by carelessness. If you touch a bare wire connected to the mains, a current can flow through you, causing a fatal shock. The other main danger is the risk of fire if things overheat.

Tap water conducts electricity and can increase the risk of an electrical accident.

A few sensible safety precautions will reduce the danger.

NEVER use appliances with frayed cables or if the cables are repaired with tape.

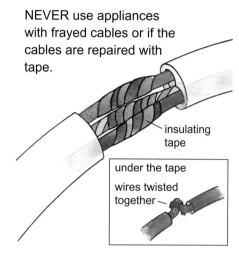

insulating tape

under the tape
wires twisted together

NEVER use mains appliances in the bathroom.

NEVER touch sockets or switches with wet hands.

NEVER pull a plug out by the cable.

pull

NEVER overload a socket.

NEVER leave a kettle lead switched on when disconnected from the kettle.

Question 1   2

Fuses

Sometimes a fault in a circuit produces a very large electric current. This is dangerous. A current that is too big can damage electrical appliances and cause a fire.

A **fuse** is used in a circuit to stop the current getting too big. This is the circuit symbol for a fuse.

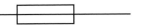

A fuse has a piece of wire inside it called fuse wire. If the current gets too big, the fuse wire gets hot and melts. When the fuse wire melts, the circuit is broken and the current stops flowing. If you look up the word 'fuse' in a dictionary you will see it has several different meanings. One of them is 'to melt'.

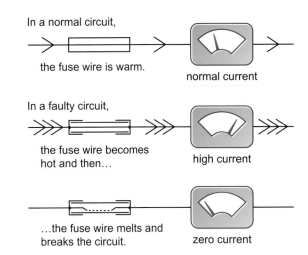

In a normal circuit, the fuse wire is warm. normal current

In a faulty circuit, the fuse wire becomes hot and then… high current

…the fuse wire melts and breaks the circuit. zero current

Question 3

Mains plugs have three pins, called terminals. If you look inside a mains plug, there are three different colours of wire.

- The blue wire goes to the neutral terminal.
- The green-and-yellow wire goes to the earth terminal.
- The brown wire goes to the live terminal.

The live terminal is the one the electric current is delivered through. The fuse is connected to the live terminal so that the current will stop if the fuse melts.

Fuses have different current ratings. The fuse wire will get hot and melt if the current through it is bigger than its rating. When the fuse wire melts and breaks, we say the fuse 'blows'. This sounds like the fuse explodes but it just means the wire has melted! The fuse drawn here has a current rating of 5 A. If a current of more than 5 A flows then the fuse will blow.

Different things use different sizes of fuse. Appliances are fitted with a fuse of a size that makes the fuse the weakest link in the circuit. The wire to the reading lamp, for example, might carry 5 A safely so the fuse must have a lower rating than this. If you put a 13 A fuse in a reading lamp then the wire has a lower rating than the fuse. If there is a fault in the lamp, the wire will catch fire and melt before the fuse blows.

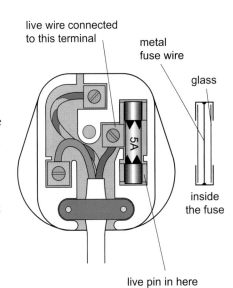

live wire connected to this terminal

metal fuse wire

glass

5 A

inside the fuse

live pin in here

Household appliance	Typical fuse size
kettle	13 A
reading lamp	3 A
hairdryer	5 A

Review your work

Question 4   5   6

Summary ➡

You should already know | Outcomes | Keywords

Using electric currents has transformed the way people live. The first electric light bulb that would last for a reasonable length of time was invented in 1879. By 1900, there were still very few homes in the UK that used electricity for lighting. By 2000, it would have been hard to find a home that did not have electric lights. Now, we use electricity for many more things. We use it to transfer energy from place to place, and to make hundreds of different things work.

We use electricity for communication and information transfer in television, telephones, the internet and computing. These are only a few examples.

However, electricity can kill. It is also quite difficult to make safely on a large scale.

There are some problems to solve because of our high use of electricity.

Some are practical problems.

- How can we make enough electricity to meet the demand?
- How can we get the electricity from one place to another safely?
- How can people use electricity in their homes and stay safe?

Solving these problems is not only a matter of science. It also involves **moral and ethical questions** because different solutions have different effects on how people live and on the environment.

- Power stations contribute to global warming. Should we build more of them just because people want to use electricity or should we limit their use of it?
- Do power lines near homes make people ill?
- Does it matter if people electrocute themselves by being careless? Is it their own fault or should the design engineers make it impossible to happen by accident?

Applying science to solve these problems is called **technology** or **engineering**.

Using science has ethical and moral implications.

Electric lights like these have only been in common use for the past 70 years.

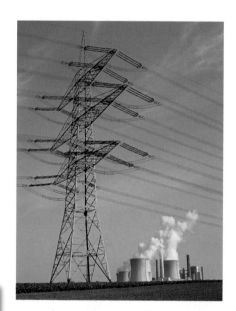

Large power stations produce electricity and cables carry the electricity all over the country.

Question 1 | 2 | 3

Assessing the risk

When you do an experiment in science, you must always assess the risks. This means thinking about all the things that could harm people or equipment. These are called **hazards**. You then work out what to do about each hazard with questions like

- Can I get the same result a different way with less hazard?
- How do I do this in a way that reduces the hazard?

In electricity experiments at school, the answers to these questions will be things like:

- use a battery or low voltage power supply for the experiment rather than the mains;
- check that the circuit is connected correctly before it is turned on.

In the home and around the country, it is not as simple as that. Scientists and engineers need to answer questions like these.

- How far away from the houses must the power lines be?
- How high up should the power lines be?
- Should people be allowed to fit their own plugs and fuses?
- What size of voltage should we supply to peoples' homes?

In the EU, the voltage supplied to homes is between 220 V and 240 V. The supply voltage to homes in North America and the Caribbean is 110 V. This lower voltage is much safer. It is less likely to give a fatal shock if someone touches a bare wire. However, if you use the lower voltage, you need to use higher currents. This increases the risk of electricity causing a fire. Whether you supply electricity at 240 V or 110 V is about the balance between the risk of shocks and the risk of fire.

This engineer has assessed the risk. The strap from his wrist reduces the hazard of a spark from his body damaging the computer chips.

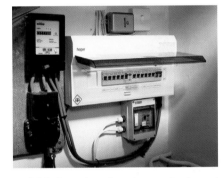

This fuse box has been designed to reduce hazards. It uses switches that can be reset. The user cannot touch any part carrying electricity.

Supply voltage	Reducing the risk	Disadvantages
110 V	Use thick wires so the high currents do not get them too hot.	Thick wires are a lot more expensive than thin ones.
240 V	Use well designed plugs and appliances so that people cannot get shocks	Safer designs adds to the cost of appliances.

Working out the balance between the risk of fire and the risk of fatal shock involves moral and ethical decisions and affects the way people live.

A 13A plug from the UK, designed for maximum safety for the user.

Question 4 5 6

7K.1 About forces (HSW)

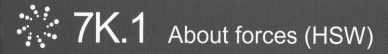

You should already know

Outcomes

Keywords

What do forces do?

In everyday life there are many different examples of **force**. They are all **pushes** or **pulls**. A force can make something start moving, it can speed things up or it can slow things down. A force can also cause something to change its direction.

You can show the direction of a force on a diagram with an arrow. In these diagrams, the forces are shown with blue arrows.

pull

The drawer moves in the same direction as you pull it.

push

A push makes the buggy start moving.

bigger pushing force

The buggy moves faster.

pull

buggy slows from this speed

to this

A force in the opposite direction slows the buggy down.

The force from the player's head changes the direction of the ball.

Question 1 2

If two forces are the same size, we sometimes call them equal forces. If equal forces act in opposite directions, they cancel each other out. This is what happens in a tug of war or when you hold up a weight.

Pairs of equal and opposite forces are sometimes called **balanced forces**. If something is still and the forces acting on it are balanced then it stays still. Things only speed up, slow down or change direction when the forces are not balanced.

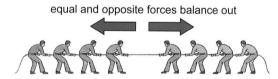

equal and opposite forces balance out

Balanced forces.

lifting force of arm muscles

weight of dumb-bell

Question 3

Forces can be balanced when things are moving

An unbalanced force can speed something up or slow something down. If the forces on a moving object are balanced then it does not speed up or slow down. It keeps moving at a steady speed.

This is what happens to a parachutist. After they have fallen with an open parachute for a short while, the drag force of the air balances the force down. They fall at a steady speed that is slow enough for them to hit the ground safely.

A similar thing happens when someone rides a bike. As the cyclist moves through the air, the air produces a force that tries to slow the cyclist down. If the force pushing the cyclist forwards from the action of pedalling is the same size as the force from the air, the forces are balanced and the cyclist goes at a steady speed.

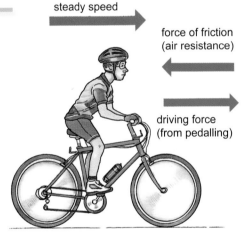

force of friction (drag)

steady speed

force of gravity (weight)

steady speed

force of friction (air resistance)

driving force (from pedalling)

Question 4 / **5**

Measuring forces

We measure forces in **newtons**.

Situation	Approximate force in newtons
pull of the Earth on a kilogram of sugar	10
weight of a 20 stone sumo wrestler	1 300
force on a racing car speeding up from 0 mph to 60 mph in 5 seconds	40 000

One newton is the size of force you need to lift a small apple. You need about 5 N to pick up a cup of tea.

You can measure the size of a force by using a newtonmeter.

A newtonmeter has a spring inside it. Different forces stretch the spring by different amounts.

To measure large forces, you use a newtonmeter with a spring made from thick wire. The yellow newtonmeter has a thick wire so it measures large forces.

To measure small forces, you use a newtonmeter with a spring made of thin wire. The green newtonmeter has a thin wire so it measures smaller forces than the yellow newtonmeter.

Another name for a newtonmeter is a forcemeter.

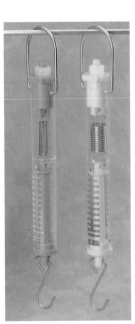

Question 6 / **7**

7K.2 Weight

The Earth pulls things towards it

When something is dropped, it falls towards the centre of the Earth. The force that pulls it down is called **weight**. The arrows in this diagram show the direction of this force on objects at different places around the Earth.

Weight is a force that happens whether or not the Earth and the object touch each other. You measure the weight of something when you hang it on a forcemeter. The diagram shows the weight of some typical objects in newtons.

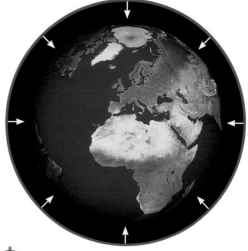

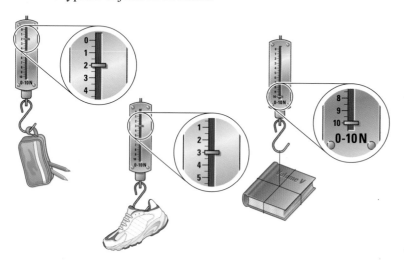

Question 1 **2**

Isaac Newton and gravity

In the 17th century, Isaac Newton worked out that every object attracted every other object with a force called **gravity**. Gravity only produces a small force compared with other forces if the objects are small. You only really notice gravity when one of the objects involved is very heavy like the Earth or the Moon.

The force of gravity between two apples is far too small to notice but the force between an apple and the Earth is obvious. If you hold an apple over the Earth's surface and let go, the force of gravity will make it fall down.

The force of gravity between two small objects is too small to notice.

The Earth has a very big mass. So there is a large force of gravity between the Earth and other objects.

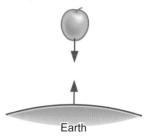

Earth

Question 3

The idea of the force of gravity attracting everything is very important. Newton used it to explain how all the planets and moons move in the Solar System, how tides happen, what a comet is and many other things that people did not understand. His idea is still used today to plan space flights.

Weight and mass

Mass tells you how much stuff something is made of. Mass is measured in kilograms. This is confusing because, in everyday language, we use the word 'weight' to mean 'mass'. When you buy apples in a supermarket, you pay for them by the kilogram. In everyday language, people call the number of kilograms 'the weight'. In science this is wrong. The number of kilograms is always the mass of something.

In science, the word 'weight' always refers to a force. Weight is the pull of gravity on something that has a mass.

The Earth pulls a 1 kilogram bag of sugar with a force of about 10 N. We say the weight of the sugar is 10 newtons.

Object	Mass (g)	Mass (kg)	Weight (N)
DVD in case	100	0.1	1
classical guitar	1400	1.4	14
litre bottle of squash	1000	1	10
11 stone person	69300	69.3	693

The weights and masses of some things on the Earth.

The Earth's gravity is about six times bigger than the Moon's.

 Question 4 **5**

The weight of something is usually balanced by another force in the everyday world.

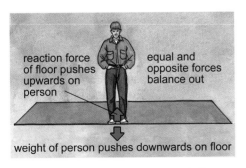

reaction force of floor pushes upwards on person

equal and opposite forces balance out

weight of person pushes downwards on floor

People don't fall through floors.

The weight of the book is balanced by a push from the table.

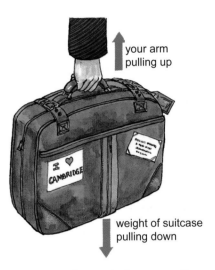

your arm pulling up

weight of suitcase pulling down

The two forces balance, so the suitcase stays still.

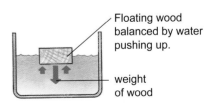

Floating wood balanced by water pushing up.

weight of wood

Question 6

Check your progress

You should already know

Outcomes

Keywords

Friction is a very important force in our lives. You cannot walk without friction. Clothes would fall apart without friction and shoelaces would be impossible to tie. Screws and nails would just drop out of whatever they were in. Our world would fall apart without friction.

When you walk, you push your foot backwards. The friction force between your foot and the floor moves you forwards. This happens because the floor does not move. If you try the same thing off a skateboard then you won't get very far, because the skateboard moves back. There is no push from it to make you go forwards. The wheels of the skateboard reduce the friction to a very low level.

Places where friction happens

Friction happens when things try to move past each other. It is a force you get when things touch. Friction happens before things start sliding and when they are actually sliding.

Look at the pictures of Eric and Sonja pushing the box.

push of foot on floor when you step forwards

push of floor on foot moves you forwards
Your foot does not slide.

push of foot when you step forwards

The board moves back.

Eric and Sonja push the box. It doesn't move.

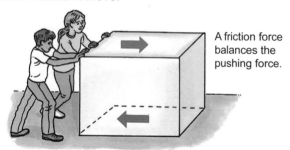

A friction force balances the pushing force.

The friction force happens where the box touches the floor.

Eric and Sonja push harder. The box still doesn't move.

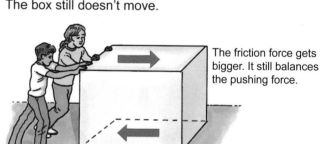

The friction force gets bigger. It still balances the pushing force.

The friction force is in the opposite direction to the push.

Eric and Sonja push harder still. Now the box moves.

movement

The friction force can't get any bigger. The pushing force is now bigger than the friction force. There is an unbalanced force. So the box moves.

Question 1 2 3

Reducing friction

Friction is a problem when surfaces need to move over each other. You can reduce friction in three ways:

- make the surfaces smooth;
- put a **lubricant** like oil on them;
- make the moving parts so that they roll rather than slide.

Rollers reduce friction. This idea is used in the hub of a wheel. A wheel turns on sets of ball bearings. These reduce friction because they roll rather than slide. You can also reduce the friction by adding oil. We say that the oil lubricates the moving parts.

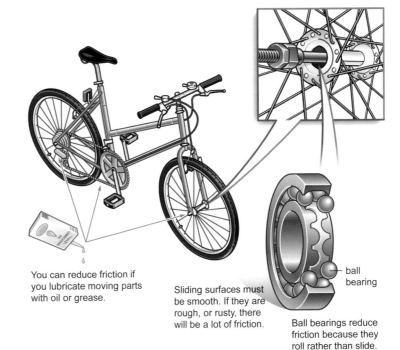

You can reduce friction if you lubricate moving parts with oil or grease.

Sliding surfaces must be smooth. If they are rough, or rusty, there will be a lot of friction.

ball bearing

Ball bearings reduce friction because they roll rather than slide.

Question 4   5

Another friction force

The friction force when something slides through air or a liquid is called **drag**.

Drag can be very useful. If you want to slow down the fall of an object, you use a parachute to provide a large drag force.

This idea is also used by some plants to spread their seeds. The seeds have small wings or fine hairs coming from them to act like a sort of parachute. The drag of the air slows down the fall of the seeds and they can be dispersed by the wind. Seeds can travel a long way on the wind before they hit the ground. This means that the new plant growing from the seed will not be competing with the original plant for food.

Drag also makes it harder to speed things up.

Racing cars have a shape that makes the drag as low as possible. The same idea is also used to design the shapes of cars and vans. A car with a shape that moves through the air easily does not use as much petrol as a car of the same size going at the same speed with a shape that gives more drag.

We say that the shape that goes through the air with less drag is more **streamlined**.

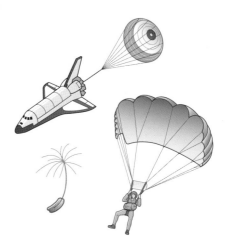

movement

air resistance

The car has to push air out of the way.

The shape of this car gives it a lot of air resistance.

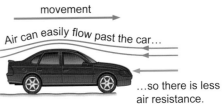

movement

Air can easily flow past the car…

…so there is less air resistance.

We say this car has a streamlined shape.

Question 6   7

You should already know

Outcomes

Keywords

Using the brakes

Friction is used to stop things moving. Brakes and tyres are designed to make good use of friction.

When you want to stop a bike or car, you use the brakes. The brakes push on the wheels and produce a friction force. The friction force slows the wheels down.

Even if you have good brakes, you need a good grip on the road as well. When you use the brakes, you produce a friction force between the road and the wheel. If your tyres do not have a good grip or the road is too slippery, the friction force will be too small and you will skid.

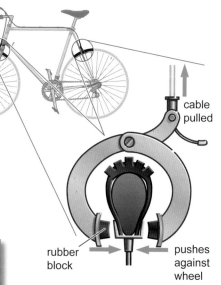

cable pulled

rubber block

pushes against wheel

How a bicycle brake works.

This tyre is old and very worn.

This tyre is brand new.

Did you know that a bald tyre actually grips a dry road better than a new tyre? But there is a problem when the road is even slightly damp or wet. On damp roads, the bald tyre will slip all over the place and cause accidents. There is a law against driving around with bald tyres.

Question 1   2

Speed and stopping

When you ride a bike or travel in a car, you describe how fast you travel by the **speed**. Speed tells you how far you go in a certain time. A speed of 30 miles per hour (mph) means that you would travel 30 miles in 1 hour if you kept going at that speed. A speed of 20 km/h means that you would travel 20 kilometres in 1 hour if you kept going at that speed.

The maximum speed that traffic is allowed to go at in built-up areas is 30 mph, which is about 48 km/h or 13 m/s.

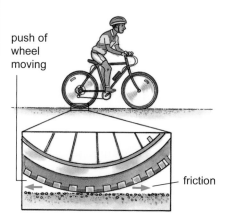

push of wheel moving

friction

The friction between a rubber tyre and a rough road surface moves the bike forwards.

	Speed in mph	Speed in km/h	Speed in m/s
Walking	4	6.4	1.8
Cycling	12	almost 20	5.4
Cheetah running	70	113	31.3

Some typical speeds in miles per hour, kilometres per hour and metres per second.

Question 3

The speed of a car affects how long it takes to stop.

The faster you are going, the longer it takes to stop.

The blue stripe shows the distance you travel while you are just thinking about stopping. If a driver is tired, affected by medicines, under the influence of alcohol or drugs, on a mobile phone, or even just distracted by a conversation with a passenger, the **thinking distance** can be a lot longer because reactions are slower.

The red stripe shows the distance you travel once you start to brake. If the road is slippery or the tyres are worn or if you start to skid then the braking distance will be a lot greater.

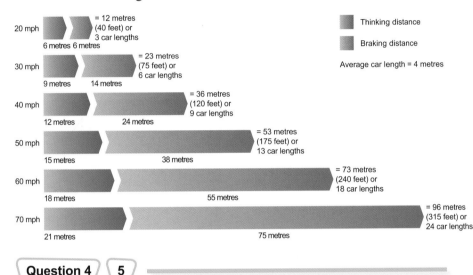

This chart is taken from the Highway Code.

Question 4 / **5**

Showing a bike ride on a graph

You can use a graph to draw a picture of a journey. The graph in the diagram is called a distance–time graph. It shows a journey for a cyclist.

In section A, the bike is moving at a steady speed.

Section B also represents a steady speed but it is a lower speed than A because of the hill, so the slope of the graph is not as steep.

At C, the cyclist has stopped for a rest and so the graph is flat.

At D, the graph has a shallow slope because the cyclist is pushing the bike at walking speed.

E is a very steep section because the bike is moving at high speed.

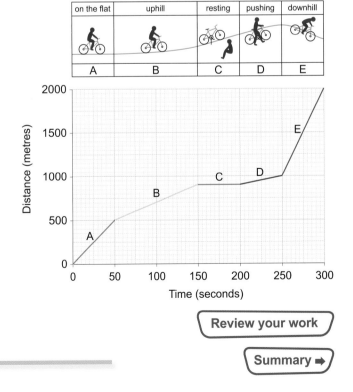

Review your work

Question 6

Summary ➡

You should already know | Outcomes | Keywords

Galileo and falling objects

Galileo was an Italian scientist and mathematician. He lived from 1564 to 1642, and was one of the first scientists to use **experiments** and **mathematics** to answer questions and to test ideas. This was a new way of working in 1600. Until then, virtually all scientists tried to explain things by arguing about them. They also tried to make everything fit in with the ideas of Greek and Arab philosophers from almost 2000 years earlier.

One idea that came from the Greeks was that heavy objects fell faster than light objects. Galileo did experiments to test this idea as well as many others. He proved that it was wrong using the observations from his experiments. He was also very good at explaining things, and he worked out a way of proving that the idea was wrong with words.

He is supposed to have tested the idea by dropping a large cannon ball and a small metal ball at the same time from the top of the tower of Pisa to show that both balls hit the ground at the same time. It is unlikely that he actually did this but we do know that he tested the idea in other ways with pendulums and by rolling a ball down a plane.

Question 1 | 2

Testing the ideas

Galileo thought that a feather falls more slowly than a coin because of drag from the air. He could not test this because he did not have a pump that could empty the air from a tube. However, he did describe how it might be done. Many years later, Isaac Newton carried out Galileo's experiment and found that he was right. In 1969, Neil Armstrong (the first man to walk on the Moon) also repeated the experiment. He dropped a hammer and a feather side by side on the Moon. The hammer and feather fell at exactly the same rate.

In science, we use evidence from observations and experiments.

Sometimes there is more than one way of approaching a scientific problem.

The Leaning Tower of Pisa.

Astronauts tested some of our ideas about motion on the Moon.

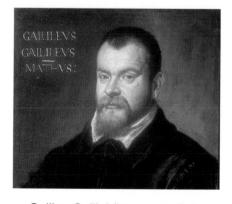

Galileo Galilei (known as Galileo) at the age of 42, in 1606.

Isaac Newton and gravity

Galileo described how things fall but it was Isaac Newton (1642 to 1727) who explained why. Newton was one of the best mathematicians there has ever been. He was also very interested in astronomy. He used mathematics to explain many things including how things move. By the age of 24, he had worked out the idea of **gravity**. This explained why things fall and how moons go round planets and planets go round the Sun.

Part of Newton's big idea was that the law of gravity was the same for everything: planets, moons, stars and an apple falling from a tree. He tested this idea. He used the time the Moon took to go round the Earth and the distance from the Earth to the Moon to work out how fast an apple falls to the Earth. The result of his experiments did not match the calculation. He thought that his theory must be wrong.

About 6 years later, the astronomer John Flamsteed gave Newton a better estimate for the distance from the Earth to the Moon. This time, the calculation for the fall of an apple worked out. It looked like Newton had got it right after all!

The idea that the same laws applied on Earth and in the heavens completely changed the way people thought and behaved. Newton's ideas and discoveries are one of the starting points for the **technological culture** we live in today.

Question 3 **4**

Light and gravity

In 1905, Albert Einstein produced a theory called <u>relativity</u>. The theory explained gravity in a different way to Newton. Because of that, most scientists thought the theory was wrong. They wanted to test it.

One prediction was that gravity bends light very slightly. In 1919, astronomers measured the bending of light in a solar eclipse in Africa. This showed that Einstein's prediction was correct.

Another result from this theory is the most famous formula in science: $E=mc^2$. This formula led to the discovery of nuclear power and **atomic weapons**. Einstein's theory has had a big impact on the politics

> The use of nuclear power and atomic weapons raise big moral and ethical questions about the use of science. Einstein warned people about this before atomic weapons or nuclear power had been made to work.

Question 5 **6**

The force of gravity between two apples is very small. This is because they don't have much mass.

mass = 100g   mass = 100g

The force of gravity between an apples and the Earth is quite large. This is because the Earth has a very large mass.

mass = 100g

Earth
mass = billions of tonnes

Gravity is a force that attracts all masses to each other.

Woolsthorpe Manor, Lincolnshire. An ancestor of the apple tree here is supposed to have inspired Newton's ideas on gravity.

Technological culture

Things like air travel, road transport, anything that uses light (including lasers), accurate clocks and watches, anything to do with satellites (including television), and mobile phones can all be traced back to Isaac Newton in some way.

You should already know | Outcomes | Keywords

Every day the Sun rises in the **East**. It moves across the sky during the day and sets in the **West**. There are two ways of explaining this:

1 the Sun goes round the Earth once every day;
2 the Earth spins round once every day.

For many centuries most people thought this was because the Sun travels around the Earth. Some people disagreed. In the 16th century, a Polish monk called Nicolaus Copernicus put forward the idea that, if the Sun stayed still and the Earth spun, we would see the same effect. This is the correct explanation.

Imagine there was a giant stick right through the centre of the Earth from the North Pole to the South Pole. The line of the stick is called the Earth's **axis**. The Earth spins around this axis. It makes one complete turn every 24 hours. 24 hours is called a day. This explains why the Sun rises in the East and sets in the West. It also explains some other things we can observe.

It explains why we get day and night. Only the parts of the Earth's surface facing the Sun are lit. On those parts, it is daytime. The parts of the Earth's surface that are facing away from the Sun are in darkness; it is night time there.

The Earth is never still. There are always parts of the Earth's surface that are moving into the light and other parts moving out of the light.

In the first picture below, the UK is facing the Sun and so it is daytime there. Australia is facing away from the Sun and it is night time there. India is just entering the dark side, so it is dusk.

12 hours later, in the second picture below, it is night time in the UK and daytime in Australia. In India, it is getting light, so it is dawn.

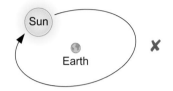

The Sun orbits the Earth

OR

The Earth spins in front of the Sun.

Two ways of explaining daytime and night time.

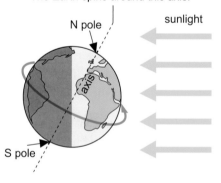

The Earth spins around this axis.

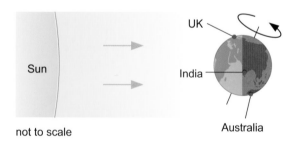

not to scale

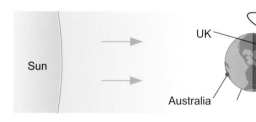

not to scale

Question 1 / 2

The Earth spins. At the same time, the Earth travels around the Sun.
The path of the Earth round the Sun is called its **orbit**. We say that the
Earth orbits the Sun. It takes the Earth 1 year to orbit the Sun.

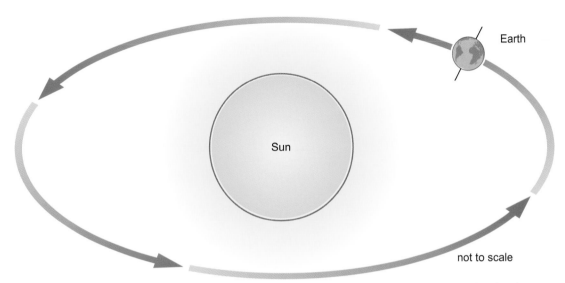

not to scale

The Earth takes a year to orbit the Sun.

In the time it takes the Earth to go once around the Sun, the Earth spins
365¼ times on its axis. This means that a year is actually 365¼ days long!
Because calendars only work in whole numbers of days, we say that a
year is 365 days long. This makes a year on the calendar one-quarter of a
day short. To make up for this, we add a day to the end of February every
4 years. This is called a leap year. This is included at the end of the old
poem to remember the numbers of days in the months:

> Thirty days hath September, April, June and November.
>
> All the rest have 31, except February alone,
>
> Which has 28 days and 29 in a leap year.

2004, 2008 and 2012 are all leap years.

Mon	Tue	Wed	Thu	Fri	Sat	Sun
				1	2	3
4	5	6	7	8	9	10
11	12	13	14	15	16	17
18	19	20	21	22	23	24
25	26	27	28	29		

Here is the calendar for February in 2008.

Question 3 4 5

You should already know   Outcomes   Keywords

As we go through a year, things change. In the UK, the average temperature in the day goes up and then back down as the year goes from January to December. The number of hours of daylight in a day also goes up and then back down. The longest day in the UK is on the 21st of June every year, with about 16 hours of daylight. The shortest day is on the 21st of December with about 8 hours of daylight.

We can explain these changes because the Earth's axis is **tilted**. This means that the Earth's axis is at an angle to one side, so that different parts of the Earth are towards the Sun or away from it during the year.

We call the top half of the Earth the northern **hemisphere** and the bottom half the southern hemisphere. When your hemisphere is tilted towards the Sun, you are in summer. When your hemisphere is tilted away from the Sun, you are in winter.

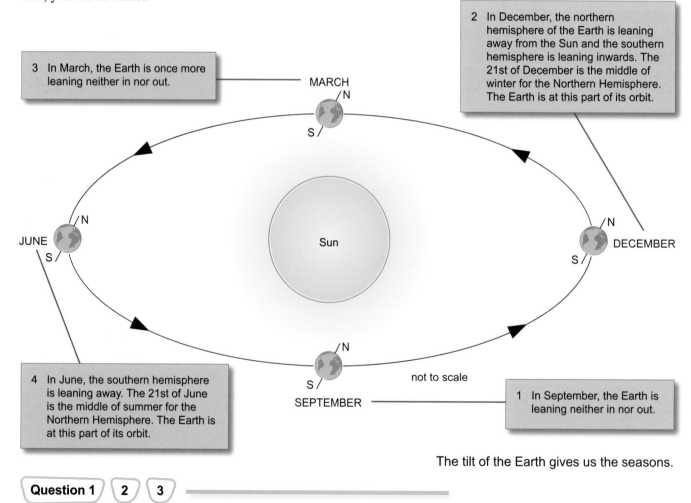

3 In March, the Earth is once more leaning neither in nor out.

2 In December, the northern hemisphere of the Earth is leaning away from the Sun and the southern hemisphere is leaning inwards. The 21st of December is the middle of winter for the Northern Hemisphere. The Earth is at this part of its orbit.

4 In June, the southern hemisphere is leaning away. The 21st of June is the middle of summer for the Northern Hemisphere. The Earth is at this part of its orbit.

1 In September, the Earth is leaning neither in nor out.

The tilt of the Earth gives us the seasons.

Question 1   2   3

Why it is warmer in summer

One of the main differences between summer and winter is temperature. The tilt of the Earth's axis and the curve of the Earth's surface are the causes of this.

In summer, the rays of light from the Sun shine on a smaller surface area than they do in winter. This means that the rays are more concentrated and they have more effect. The part of the Earth that is tilted towards the Sun becomes warmer.

In winter, the Sun's rays are shining on a larger surface area than they do in summer. The Sun's rays are less concentrated, so the Earth's surface does not get so warm.

There is a second reason for summer being warmer than winter. In summer, daytime lasts longer. This means that the Sun's rays have longer to heat the surface. This helps to raise the temperature.

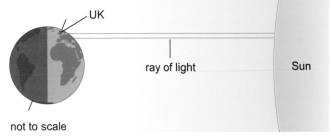

In June.

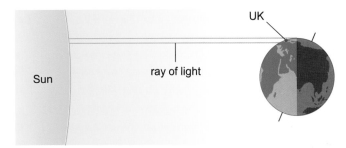

In December.

Question 4

Why we have more hours of daylight in summer

The second main difference between winter and summer is the length of daylight in a day. It takes 24 hours for the Earth to turn once on its axis, but the number of hours of daylight varies through the year.

At any time, half of the Earth faces the Sun and the other half is hidden from it. For the half facing the Sun, it is day. For the hidden half, it is night.

The Earth's axis is at an angle to the line that divides day from night.

Because of the tilt of the Earth's axis, in June the northern hemisphere spends more time in daylight than in darkness as it spins. It is summer there. When you look at the Sun in the summer it appears higher in the sky than it does in the winter.

In December, the northern hemisphere spends less time in daylight than in darkness as it spins. It is winter there. The Sun appears lower in the sky.

There is a small section of the Earth around the North Pole where the Sun never rises on the 21st of December each year and where the Sun never sets on the 21st of June. It is known as 'the Land of the Midnight Sun'. On maps of the Earth, the edge of this area is shown as a line called the Arctic Circle.

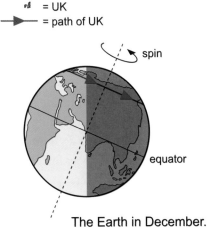

The Earth in June.

= UK
= path of UK

The Earth in December.

Question 5   **6**

You should already know ⟩ Outcomes ⟩ Keywords

When you look up at the sky on a clear night away from street lights, you can see lots of dots of light.

- Some of these are **stars**.
- Some of these are **planets**.
- Some are artificial **satellites** reflecting the sunlight.

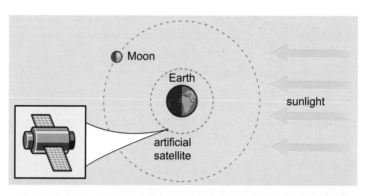

Stars

A star gives out its own light. We say that it is **luminous**. Stars are spread throughout the Universe. The nearest star to the Earth is the Sun. It looks bigger than all the other stars because it is much closer to the Earth than the others.

If you look at the stars carefully at different times in the night, they appear to move round the sky in circles. You can see this easily if you take a long exposure photograph of the sky over several hours.

If you look at the stars from somewhere in the northern hemisphere, like the UK, they all seem to move around a star called Polaris. This star is also known as the pole star.

Each star appears to move around the pole star.

This happens because the Earth's axis points at Polaris and the Earth is spinning on its axis.

Stars are massive. Our Sun is not particularly big as stars go but even its diameter is over 100 times more than the Earth's. That means that if the Sun was the size of a football then the Earth would be about the size of a peppercorn on the same scale.

Like the Sun and Moon, the stars seem to move across the sky. Only the pole star stays in the same place. This gives us further evidence that the Earth is spinning.

Things to do with the Sun are said to be **solar**. The collection of planets, including us, going around the Sun is called the **Solar System**. The next nearest star to our Sun is so far away that light from it takes 4 years to reach us. The distance to it is over a quarter of a million times the distance from the Earth to the Sun!

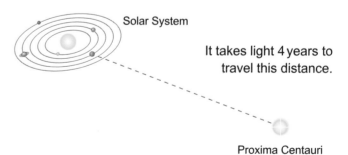

It takes light 4 years to travel this distance.

Proxima Centauri

Question 1 ⟩ 2

Planets

Some stars have planets going around them in orbits. There are nine planets orbiting the Sun if you count Pluto as a planet. The Earth is one of them. Planets are giant lumps of rock or balls of gas. They do not give out light but they can reflect it. We can only see planets because they reflect the Sun's light. The planets that are closest to the Sun (Mercury, Venus, Mars and Jupiter) can all be seen without telescopes. They just look like stars in the sky. The more distant planets (Saturn, Uranus, Neptune and Pluto) are much harder to see because they are further away. You need a telescope to look at these planets.

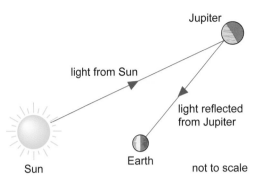

Question 3   4

The Moon

The Moon is the closest body in space to the Earth. It orbits the Earth, so it is called a <u>satellite</u> of the Earth. Like the planets, the Moon does not give out its own light; it reflects light from the Sun. Things to do with the Moon are said to be **lunar**.

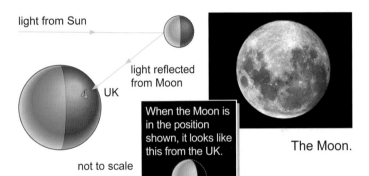

When the Moon is in the position shown, it looks like this from the UK.

The Moon.

Phases of the Moon

Half of the Moon is in sunlight and half is in darkness. We can only see the part of the Moon that is facing us. As the Moon moves round the Earth, the part of its surface that faces us is not always the part that is reflecting the Sun's light. The Moon does not produce light of its own; it is not luminous. This is why the amount we can see of the Moon varies from night to night.

The Moon takes 28 days to orbit the Earth. This is called a lunar month. The lunar month starts when we can see just a thin crescent of the Moon. We call this a New Moon.

As the Moon moves around the Earth, we see more of the side lit by the Sun. The crescent gets larger. We say that it <u>waxes</u>.

When the light side of the Moon faces us, we see a Full Moon. It looks like a disc.

As the Moon moves round, less sunlight is reflected in our direction. It starts to appear smaller again because some of the part reflecting sunlight is facing away from Earth. We say that the Moon <u>wanes</u>. The Moon becomes a crescent again. At the end of the lunar month, the side of the Moon that is in shadow faces us. The Moon disappears because the side facing us does not reflect any light from the Sun in our direction.

The stages that we see are known as the **phases** of the Moon.

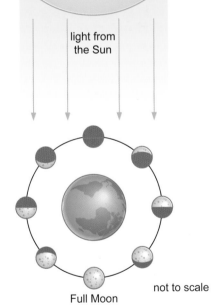

What the Moon looks like from the Earth when it is in different positions.

Question 5   6

Check your progress

You must be careful looking at the Sun. You must <u>never</u> look directly at it even wearing sunglasses. The Sun is so bright its light can permanently damage your eyes.

If you observe the Sun and the Moon from the Earth, they appear to be about the same size. But this is just an illusion. The Sun is actually 400 times bigger than the Moon. If the Sun was the size of a house, the Moon would be the size of a mouse. The diameter of the Sun is over 400 times bigger than that of the Moon. However, the Sun is nearly 400 times further away from the Earth than the Moon is. The difference in their sizes is cancelled out by the difference in their distances from the Earth. They appear to be the same size in the sky.

the setting Sun

the Moon in exactly the same direction at a different time

The Sun and the Moon look the same size.

Eclipses

Because the Moon appears to be the same size as the Sun, it can blot the Sun out if it gets into just the right position. This happens occasionally when the Moon passes between the Sun and the Earth. This is called a **solar eclipse**. The Moon casts a shadow on the surface of the Earth. The part of the Earth where the shadow falls is dark, even though it is daytime! If you are in the place where the shadow is, the Sun is hidden by the Moon.

There are two parts to the Moon's shadow. In the very middle is a complete shadow where all of the Sun is blocked out. This is called a total eclipse. This area is usually only a few miles across. Total eclipses are not very common in the UK. The last one was in August 1999 in Cornwall.

Around the edge of the total shadow, there is a part shadow where only some of the Sun is blocked out. People in this area see a **partial eclipse**. This area stretches for hundreds of miles. When the total eclipse happened in Cornwall, the partial eclipse could be seen in Yorkshire.

x = total eclipse   not to scale

An eclipse of the Sun happens when the Earth is in the Moon's shadow.

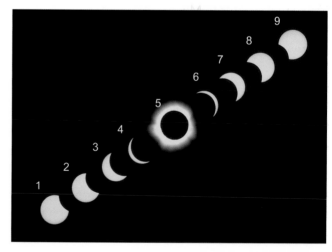
Nine photos of the stages of a total solar eclipse. Number 5 shows totality.

Question 1 2 3

Eclipses do not happen every lunar month. The orbit of the Moon around the Earth is at a slight angle compared with the orbit of the Earth around the Sun. This means that the Earth, Moon and Sun do not line up very often.

Solar eclipses do not happen very often over the same place on the Earth. Between 1724 and 1927, there were no total eclipses visible from mainland Britain.

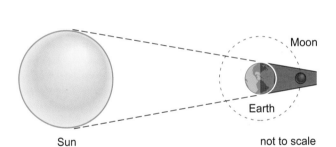

not to scale

Date	Notes
1st August 2008	partial eclipse
4th January 2011	partial eclipse in south-east England
20th March 2015	partial eclipse
11th August 2018	partial eclipse in the north of Scotland
23rd September 2090	total eclipse in Cornwall lasting 2 minutes and 10 seconds

The solar eclipses visible from the UK in this century.

Question 4

Lunar eclipses

The second type of eclipse we see from Earth is called a **lunar eclipse**. This happens when the Sun, Earth and Moon line up, with the Earth <u>between</u> the Sun and the Moon.

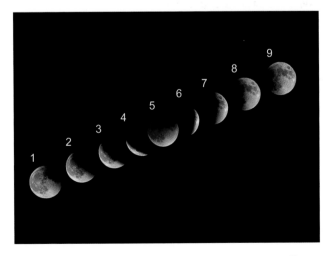

not to scale

An eclipse happens when the Moon is the Earth's shadow.

A lunar eclipse happens when the Moon has moved into the Earth's shadow.

You would expect the Moon to disappear completely because there would be no light reaching it, but this is not quite what happens. The Earth's atmosphere bends some light from the Sun around to the Moon. This means that the Moon is lit up by a faint glow. If you look at the photograph under the number 5, you can see that the Moon is a faint reddish orange colour, a bit like copper metal, when the total eclipse happens.

Again, because the Moon's orbit is at an angle to the Earth's orbit, lunar eclipses do not happen every month, but they are much more common than solar eclipses. Sometimes there are several in a year.

Question 5   **6**

Nine photos of a total lunar eclipse.

You should already know	Outcomes	Keywords

There are nine planets orbiting the Sun. The Earth is one of them. This collection of the Sun and planets is called the **Solar System**.

The telescope was invented in about 1610. Some planets can only be seen with a telescope and so they were not discovered until after then.

Planet	Discovery date
Mercury, Venus, Mars, Jupiter	known since ancient times
Saturn	known since ancient times, but the rings were discovered by Galileo in 1610 with one of the first telescopes
Uranus	1781
Neptune	1846
Pluto	1930

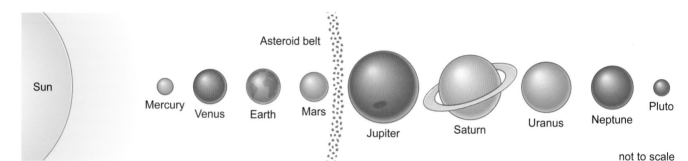

The Solar System.

Sometimes it is easier to remember a list if you can think of a saying with words that start with the same letters as the items in the list. This kind of saying is called a <u>mnemonic</u>.

My	Very	Easy	Method	Just	Speeds	Up	Naming	Planets
Mercury	Venus	Earth	Mars	Jupiter	Saturn	Uranus	Neptune	Pluto

Question 1

Mercury, Venus, Earth and Mars have a surface that is made from rock. They are called the <u>rocky planets</u>.

Jupiter, Saturn, Uranus and Neptune are large balls of gas and are called the <u>gas giants</u>.

Pluto is very small and is made of rock and ice. It is sometimes called an <u>ice dwarf</u>.

The **asteroid belt** is between Mars and Jupiter. Asteroids are rocks that are not big enough to be planets. They might be from a planet that broke up a long time ago.

Is there life on Mars?

Mars is the nearest planet to us. We have been able to send spacecraft to Mars and to put robots on its surface to do some exploration. Its surface looks like it has had water on it and we know that it has an atmosphere. If there is any water there now, it is probably deep below the surface.

Observations from telescopes and the information collected by spacecraft and robots we have sent to Mars tell us that there are no large living things there. Experiments have been done on Mars to test for small living things like bacteria.

Living things normally affect the atmosphere around them. An experiment done by one of the robots on Mars mixed Martian soil with water and nutrient in a closed container. The changes in the gases produced could be explained by simple chemical reactions. There was no evidence of life.

The gases in the atmosphere of Mars compare closely with the atmosphere the Earth would have if there was no life on it.

Gases in the atmosphere	Earth (no life)	Earth (actual)	Mars
carbon dioxide	98%	0.03%	95%
nitrogen	1.9%	79%	2.7%
oxygen	trace	21%	0.13%

If there was life on Mars a long time ago then there might be fossils to show evidence of it. We find fossils in rocks on Earth from plants, animals and even bacteria that lived and died millions of years ago. In 1996 a meteorite from Mars was found in Antarctica. Some scientists thought that it had fossils of bacteria inside. However, the fossils were 100 times smaller than similar fossils on Earth. They were probably not really fossils, just rock.

Scientists have not found any good evidence of fossils on Mars.

What about other places?

Another possible place where there might be life is on one of Jupiter's moons called Europa. Photographs from spacecraft show that there is a lot of ice on the surface and there is probably liquid water below it that could support life.

There are billions of stars in the Universe just like our Sun and many stars have planets. Even if there is intelligent life on one of them, we are not likely to find out unless we get radio signals from them, because the other stars are just too far away for our spacecraft to reach.

The surface of Mars.

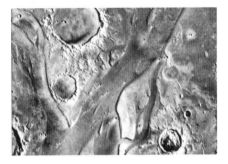

This photograph of the surface of Mars shows that it has been eroded in the past by flowing water.

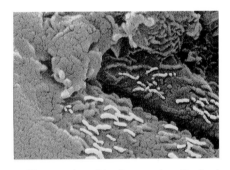

Shapes in a Martian meteorite that were thought to be fossils of bacteria.

The surface of Europa shows cracks in a surface of ice.

Review your work

Summary ➡

Question 4 5 6 7

You should already know

Outcomes

Keywords

Explaining what we see

Most people used to think that the Earth was still and that the stars and planets moved around it. A few scientists suggested other ideas. In 270 BC Aristarchus suggested that the Earth moved around the Sun, but his idea was rejected because:

- it didn't have human beings at the centre of the Universe;
- it did not explain why things did not fall off the Earth as it flew through space;
- people believed that the view of the stars would change as the Earth moved closer and further away, and this did not happen.

Copernicus suggested a similar idea in 1543. Most people rejected it for the same reasons.

In 1610, Galileo made a **telescope** and used it to look at the planets and stars. He worked out that the stars were a lot further away than people thought. This meant the view would not change if the Earth did go around the Sun. He also saw four moons going around Jupiter. He thought that this was how the Earth could go around the Sun. He started to tell everyone that Copernicus had the right idea. This got him into serious trouble with the Roman Catholic Church.

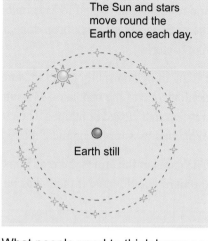

What people used to think happens.

Galileo observed the planet Jupiter through his telescope. He saw at least four moons in orbit around it.

Question 1 / 2 _____

Our view of the Universe today comes from the work of many people.

Name	Nationality	Dates	Contribution
Tycho Brahe	Danish	1546–1601	made thousands of accurate observations
Johannes Kepler	German	1571–1630	worked out laws about the way planets moved
Galileo	Italian	1564–1642	used arguments, experiments and observations to support the ideas of Copernicus
Isaac Newton	English	1642–1726	worked out the full answer and explained why it worked

Question 3 _____

Improving the view

Newton did a lot of experiments on the behaviour of light. He used his discoveries to make a much better telescope than Galileo's. His telescope used a curved mirror rather than a lens. The type of telescope he invented produces true colours. It is also easier to make one that captures a lot of light and so produces a bright image. This design of telescope is still used today to analyse the colour of light from stars.

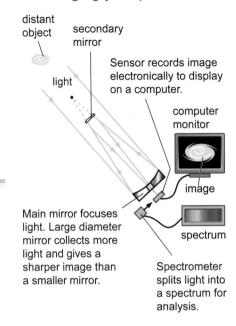

Question 4

One of the problems with a telescope on the Earth is that air pollution makes the image hazy. In 1990, a large reflecting telescope was put into space. It is called the Hubble Space Telescope, and you can find images from it on the Internet.

The development of space science has changed how we live our lives, in many ways. We use **satellites** in space for communications. Signals are transmitted up from the Earth's surface to a satellite and then sent back down again so that they reach a point around the curved surface of the Earth. This can be a big advantage to isolated communities. For example, people in remote islands like the Maldives can receive warnings of approaching tidal waves so they can escape disaster.

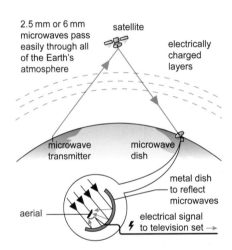

Satellites in space are also used for computer systems that tell you where you are on the Earth's surface. These global positioning system (GPS for short) devices are standard on expensive cars and can easily be fitted to cars that do not already have them.

Some satellites go around the Earth carrying telescopes to take pictures of the Earth's surface. These pictures are used in weather forecasting. You can see the results on television weather forecasts. There are websites and even programs for home computers that provide telescope photographs of the Earth's surface from space. The images are so good that you can tell if people have washing hanging on a line or not!

When we use and apply science like this, there are always **ethical questions**. Here are some examples.

Satellite dish in the Maldives.

- Are the advantages of communications and GPS systems worth the cost?
- Should we be spending billions of dollars on a telescope like Hubble just to get a clearer view of the stars?
- Is it right to spy on people from space?
- All these developments contribute to carbon emissions in some way and this contributes to global warming. Is that right?

The use of scientific ideas has ethical and moral implications.

The creative application of science can bring about changes in the way people think and behave.

Question 5 6

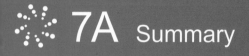

Keywords

The cytoplasm is where large numbers of chemical reactions happen.

The cell membrane controls what goes into and out of cells.

The nucleus controls the cell's activities, growth and division.

Cells have different parts, which have different jobs.

Cells divide to make new cells.

Life processes depend on chemical reactions in cells.

All living things are made of cells.

Large living things have millions of cells.

Some cells are specialised. They are adapted to the jobs that they do.

Different cells support different life processes.

Plant cells have parts that animal cells don't have.

Chloroplasts trap the light energy that plants use to make food.

Vacuoles are full of liquid cell sap in the centre of the cell.

Cell walls support plant cells.

A group of similar cells is called a tissue.

An organ is made up of several tissues.

Cells are so small that we need to use a microscope to see them.

We can draw what we see to scale.

Check your progress

Review your work

Scientific enquiry

Key ideas

1 • Living things produce young of the same kind as themselves.
We say that they reproduce.

• Different creatures reproduce in different ways.

2 • In sexual reproduction, the nuclei of a sperm and an egg cell join, or fuse. We call this fertilisation.

• Sperm and egg cells are specialised to do their jobs.

• Sperm and egg nuclei contain inherited material from the parent that made them.

3 • Women have a monthly cycle controlled by hormones. We call it the menstrual cycle. An egg cell is released and menstruation happens about once a month as part of this cycle.

• The menstrual cycle stops when a woman becomes pregnant.

4 • A fertilised egg cell divides and grows to form an embryo.
It is implanted in the uterus.

• When the embryo has grown all its main organs, we call it a fetus. The placenta supplies the needs of the fetus through the umbilical cord, and the amniotic fluid cushions it.

5 • After it is born, mammary glands (breasts) produce milk for the baby.

• Human children are dependent on their parents and other adults for a long time.

6 • The time between childhood and adulthood is called adolescence. Hormones control the changes that take place during this time.

• We call the time of sexual maturity puberty. This is when eggs and sperm are first released.

Check your progress   Review your work   Scientific enquiry

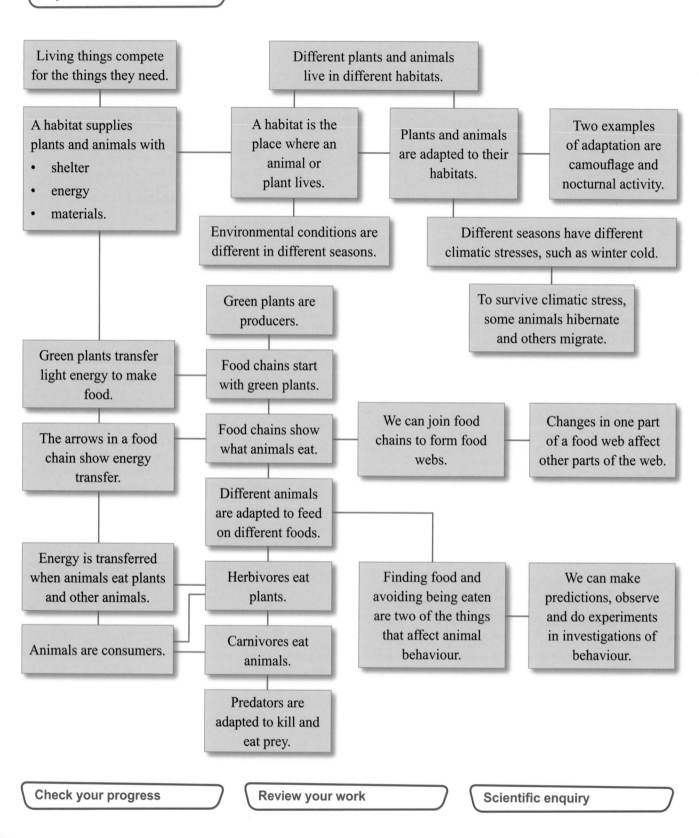

Keywords

Living things compete for the things they need.

Different plants and animals live in different habitats.

A habitat supplies plants and animals with
- shelter
- energy
- materials.

A habitat is the place where an animal or plant lives.

Plants and animals are adapted to their habitats.

Two examples of adaptation are camouflage and nocturnal activity.

Environmental conditions are different in different seasons.

Different seasons have different climatic stresses, such as winter cold.

Green plants are producers.

To survive climatic stress, some animals hibernate and others migrate.

Green plants transfer light energy to make food.

Food chains start with green plants.

The arrows in a food chain show energy transfer.

Food chains show what animals eat.

We can join food chains to form food webs.

Changes in one part of a food web affect other parts of the web.

Different animals are adapted to feed on different foods.

Energy is transferred when animals eat plants and other animals.

Herbivores eat plants.

Finding food and avoiding being eaten are two of the things that affect animal behaviour.

We can make predictions, observe and do experiments in investigations of behaviour.

Animals are consumers.

Carnivores eat animals.

Predators are adapted to kill and eat prey.

Check your progress   Review your work   Scientific enquiry

Keywords

Key ideas

- A species is one kind of living thing.

- Members of a species breed with each other to produce fertile offspring.

- Members of a species have a lot of characteristics in common.

- Individuals of the same species vary.

- Variations that pass from parents to offspring are called inherited variations.

- Differences caused by the conditions in which the plant or animal lives are called environmental variations. They are not passed on to offspring.

- Sorting things into groups is called classification. We put living things with the same characteristics in a group.

- We divide large groups into smaller groups.

- Scientists all over the world use the same classification system. This means that they all know which animals or plants they are writing about.

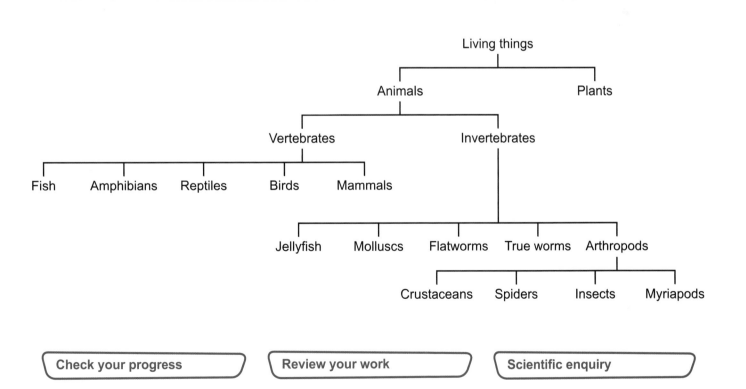

Check your progress

Review your work

Scientific enquiry

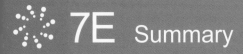

Keywords

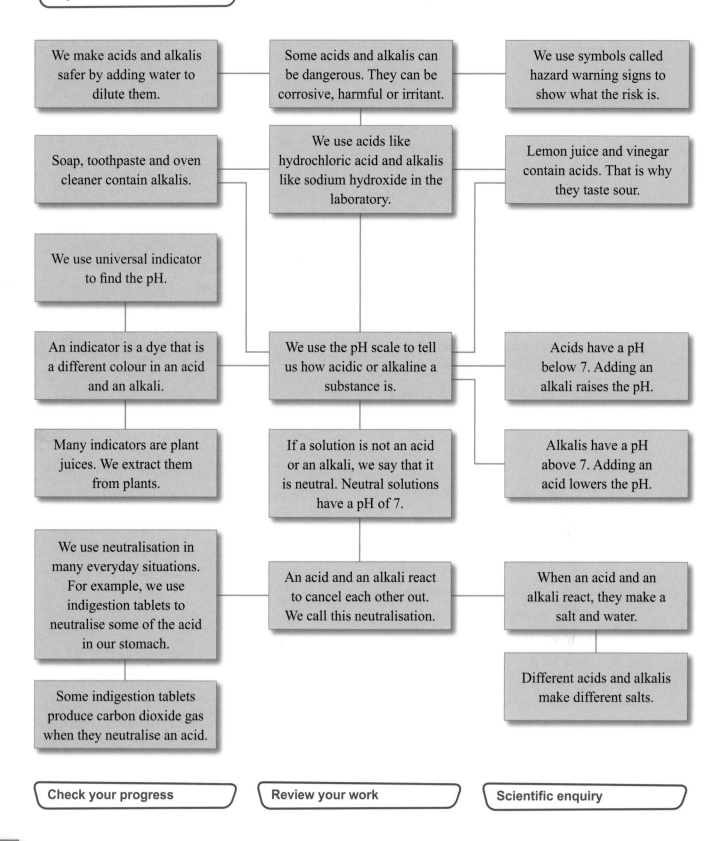

We make acids and alkalis safer by adding water to dilute them.

Some acids and alkalis can be dangerous. They can be corrosive, harmful or irritant.

We use symbols called hazard warning signs to show what the risk is.

Soap, toothpaste and oven cleaner contain alkalis.

We use acids like hydrochloric acid and alkalis like sodium hydroxide in the laboratory.

Lemon juice and vinegar contain acids. That is why they taste sour.

We use universal indicator to find the pH.

An indicator is a dye that is a different colour in an acid and an alkali.

We use the pH scale to tell us how acidic or alkaline a substance is.

Acids have a pH below 7. Adding an alkali raises the pH.

Many indicators are plant juices. We extract them from plants.

If a solution is not an acid or an alkali, we say that it is neutral. Neutral solutions have a pH of 7.

Alkalis have a pH above 7. Adding an acid lowers the pH.

We use neutralisation in many everyday situations. For example, we use indigestion tablets to neutralise some of the acid in our stomach.

An acid and an alkali react to cancel each other out. We call this neutralisation.

When an acid and an alkali react, they make a salt and water.

Some indigestion tablets produce carbon dioxide gas when they neutralise an acid.

Different acids and alkalis make different salts.

Check your progress   Review your work   Scientific enquiry

Key ideas

- In a chemical reaction, new substances are produced.

- Substances that are used up in a chemical reaction are called reactants.

- Substances that are made during a chemical reaction are called products.

- Hydrogen is produced when an acid reacts with a metal. The metal is used up. We call this corrosion.

- When a metal and an acid react, they produce a salt as well as hydrogen.

- We test for hydrogen using a lighted splint. You hear a pop if there is hydrogen.

- We can describe a chemical reaction with a word equation.

- An acid reacts with a carbonate to produce new substances. One of these is carbon dioxide.

- We use lime water to test for carbon dioxide. It is the only gas that turns lime water cloudy.

- When something burns, it reacts with oxygen.

- Your body makes carbon dioxide through the process of reproduction.

- The oxide of a substance is made when a substance burns.

- Fuels release energy when they burn.

- A fire needs oxygen from air, fuel and heat to burn. We show this as a fire triangle.

- Fossil fuels come from the remains of plants and animals that died millions of years ago.

- Fossil fuels produce carbon dioxide and water when they burn.

- Coal, oil and petrol are examples of fossil fuels.

- Methane is an example of a fossil fuel. Its common name is natural gas.

- Carbon dioxide reacts with rainwater to make acid rain.

Keywords

All the substances we can see and feel in the world are called matter.

Scientists collect observations about matter. They think of ideas to explain the observations. These ideas are called theories.

The particle model of matter

1 All matter is made up of particles.
2 The particles can be of different sizes.
3 The particles move around by themselves.
4 The particles attract each other.
5 The hotter the substance, the faster the particles move.
 Some scientists call this model the kinetic theory.

Heat travels in solids by conduction. The vibration of the particles is passed through a solid as the particles knock into each other.

In liquids, the particles are still attracted to each other but they move faster. They swap places with each other. There is a little more space between the particles.

In a gas, there is little attraction between the particles so they move freely. The particles are far apart and moving very fast.

In solids, strong forces hold the particles together so they vibrate, but do not change places. There is little space between particles.

Solids and liquids are difficult to compress, but gases compress easily. This is because gases have large gaps between the particles.

Expansion means getting bigger. Solids expand slightly; liquids expand more and gases expand a great deal. During expansion the particles move further apart.

Solids don't flow because the forces between the particles are strong. Gases and liquids flow because the forces between particles are much weaker.

Substances can be sorted into three groups: solids, liquids and gases. These three groups are called the three states of matter.

If you heat a solid, the particles can break away from each other and the solid melts.

Heating particles in a liquid makes them escape as a gas. This is evaporation.

Particles spread out because they are moving We call this diffusion.

Check your progress   Review your work   Scientific enquiry

Keywords

Distillation uses a piece of equipment called a condenser.

The solute particles travel different distances and produce a chromatogram.

A solute can be separated from a solution by evaporation.

Distillation is evaporation followed by condensation.

Chromatography works when solute particles are attracted to water particles.

A solvent can be separated from a solution by distillation.

A mixture of solutes can be separated by chromatography.

A solution forms when a solute dissolves in a solvent.

Solubility is a measure of how soluble a solid is.

Solids that are soluble will dissolve.

Sodium chloride is one example of a soluble solid.

When you measure solubility, you must state:
- the mass of the solvent;
- the mass of the solute;
- the temperature.

Solutions are mixtures.

Something is pure when it contains a single substance and not a mixture of substances.

Solids that are insoluble will not dissolve.

A saturated solution is formed when no more solid will dissolve in the solution.

When a solute dissolves in a solvent, the total mass is the mass of the solute added to the mass of the solvent. This is called conservation of mass.

Insoluble solids are separated from a liquid by filtration.

Check your progress

Review your work

Scientific enquiry

Keywords

Key ideas

- We need energy to make things happen. It is measured in joules.

- There are different types of energy, such as kinetic energy and heat energy.

- Fuels are very important in our lives. We use many different fuels.

- The energy that fuels release is useful for transport, heating, cooking and making electricity.

- Fossil fuels are made from the remains of plants and animals that died millions of years ago.

- Fossil fuels will run out. They are non-renewable.

- We use fossil fuels to make most of our electricity.

- It is important to save fossil fuels because they are running out and because burning them contributes to acid rain and global warming.

- It takes 1 J to lift a 100 g mass through 1 m.

- 1 kilojoule is 1000 joules.

- Renewable energy resources such as wind energy won't run out as long as the Sun keeps shining.

- Most renewable energy resources depend on the Sun.

- There are lots of renewable energy resources, such as solar energy and geothermal energy.

- Renewable energy resources do not cause air pollution.

- Animals eat food to get their energy. The energy in food is measured in kilojoules or kilocalories.

- Activities that we do all need energy. We get the energy we need from the chemical energy in food.

- Plants make food using the energy in sunlight.

- All the energy in food ultimately comes from the Sun.

- We need to match the energy in our diet to the energy our bodies need to keep a constant body weight.

Check your progress   Review your work   Scientific enquiry

Keywords

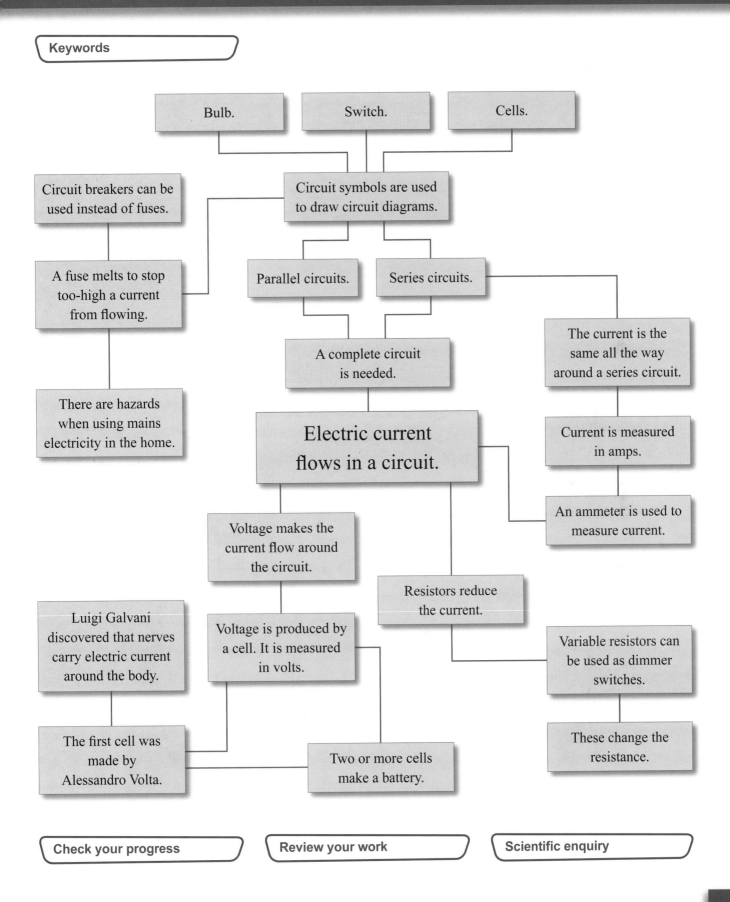

Bulb.

Switch.

Cells.

Circuit breakers can be used instead of fuses.

Circuit symbols are used to draw circuit diagrams.

A fuse melts to stop too-high a current from flowing.

Parallel circuits.

Series circuits.

The current is the same all the way around a series circuit.

There are hazards when using mains electricity in the home.

A complete circuit is needed.

Current is measured in amps.

Electric current flows in a circuit.

An ammeter is used to measure current.

Voltage makes the current flow around the circuit.

Resistors reduce the current.

Luigi Galvani discovered that nerves carry electric current around the body.

Voltage is produced by a cell. It is measured in volts.

Variable resistors can be used as dimmer switches.

The first cell was made by Alessandro Volta.

Two or more cells make a battery.

These change the resistance.

Check your progress

Review your work

Scientific enquiry

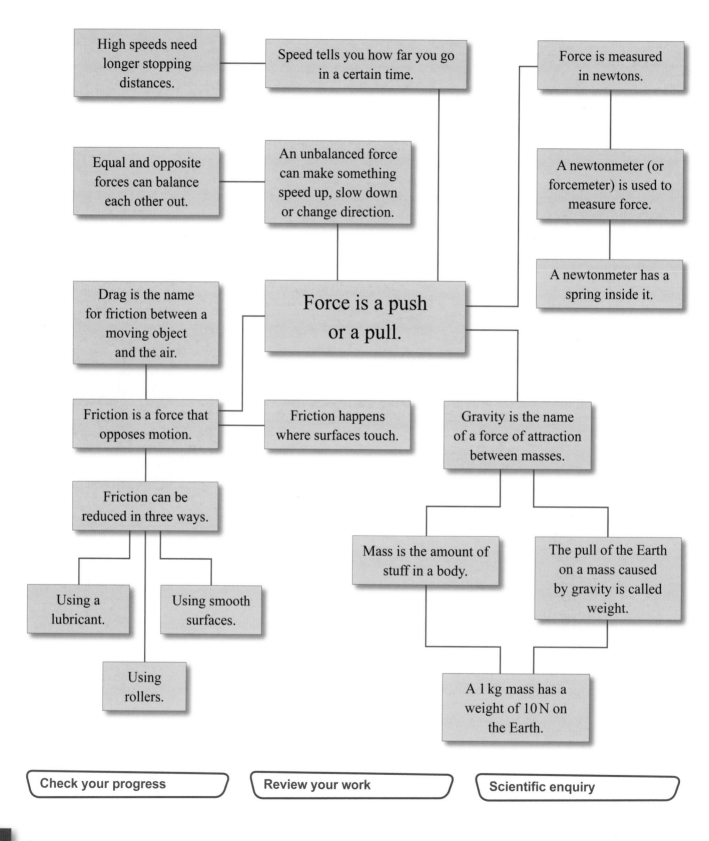

Keywords

High speeds need longer stopping distances.

Speed tells you how far you go in a certain time.

Force is measured in newtons.

Equal and opposite forces can balance each other out.

An unbalanced force can make something speed up, slow down or change direction.

A newtonmeter (or forcemeter) is used to measure force.

A newtonmeter has a spring inside it.

Drag is the name for friction between a moving object and the air.

Force is a push or a pull.

Friction is a force that opposes motion.

Friction happens where surfaces touch.

Gravity is the name of a force of attraction between masses.

Friction can be reduced in three ways.

Using a lubricant.

Using smooth surfaces.

Mass is the amount of stuff in a body.

The pull of the Earth on a mass caused by gravity is called weight.

Using rollers.

A 1 kg mass has a weight of 10 N on the Earth.

Check your progress   **Review your work**   **Scientific enquiry**

Keywords

Key ideas

- A day is the time that the Earth takes to spin once around its axis.

- A year is the time that the Earth takes to orbit once around the Sun.

- Seasons happen because the Earth is tilted on its axis. When the northern hemisphere is tilted towards the Sun, it is summer there.

- The days are longer in summer because of the tilt of the Earth's axis.

- We see stars because they are luminous.

- The stars appear to move across the night sky because the Earth is rotating.

- We see the planets because they reflect the light from the Sun. They are non-luminous.

- The Moon reflects light from the Sun. We see phases of the Moon because we can only see the side of the Moon that is lit by the Sun as the Moon orbits the Earth.

- A solar eclipse happens when the Sun, Moon and Earth line up with the Moon in the middle.

- A lunar eclipse happens when the Sun, Moon and Earth line up with the Earth in the middle.

- Nine planets are recognised in the Solar System – Mercury, Venus, Earth, Mars, Jupiter, Saturn, Uranus, Neptune and Pluto.

- These nine planets orbit the Sun and their orbits take different times to complete.

- The asteroid belt is a group of rocks orbiting the Sun between Mars and Jupiter.

- The Earth is the only planet that we know of that has life on it.

Check your progress   Review your work   Scientific enquiry

Glossary/Index

E

East a direction on the earth's surface; 90° to right of the line pointing from the South to the North; the opposite direction to West 124

egg cell female sex cell; also called an ovum 12

elastic potential energy stored in things which are stretched or squashed 92

electrical energy the energy in wires when electric current flows 92

embryo a baby in the uterus before all its organs have started to grow 15

energy energy is needed to make things happen 92

energy transfer energy moving from one place to another 34

engineering applying science to improve something 112

environmental conditions conditions such as light and temperature in the environment 24

environmental variations differences within a species caused by the environment 38

errors results or observations that are wrong; this can happen because of a mistake by the person doing the experiment, because there is something wrong with the equipment or because of a fault in the design of the experiment 70

ethical relating to ethics 100, 134

ethics a set of principles and values that may show how to behave in a particular situation 24

evaluation a statement of the strengths and weaknesses of something; for an investigation, it might include considering how well the data supports what has been found out and any improvements that could be made 60

evaporating a liquid changing into a gas 76, 82, 86

evidence observations and measurements on which scientists and others base theories 10

expansion when a substance gets bigger because its particles speed up and move further apart 78

experimenting one way of investigating or finding out what happens 10

experiments investigations to find out information, in which variables are controlled and measured to make the investigation fair 122

experimenting one way of investigating or finding out what happens 10

F

family tree a diagram to show how people are related to each other 38

fertilisation when a male sex cell joins with a female sex cell to start a new plant or animal 12, 15

fetus a baby in the uterus whose organs are all growing 15, 19

filtration separating a liquid from an undissolved solid by passing it through small holes, usually in paper 82

fire triangle the three things, fuel, heat and oxygen, needed to make a fire 68

fish a group of vertebrates that lives in water and gets oxygen through its gills 44

food chain a diagram showing what animals eat 34

food web a diagram showing what eats what in a habitat 34

force a push or a pull 114

fossil fuels a fuel formed from the remains of plants and animals from millions of years ago 68, 94

freezing when a liquid cools and becomes solid 76

friction a force when two surfaces rub past each other; it acts in the opposite direction to the direction in which something is moving 118

fuels substances that burn to release energy 68, 92

fuse (in biology) join together; the nucleus of a sperm fuses with the nucleus of an egg cell during fertilisation 12

fuse (in physics) a device that melts if too great an electric current passes through it 110

G

gas a substance that spreads out (diffuses) to fill all the space available, but can be compressed into a smaller volume 72

genus a classification group; it consists of a number of species; the first part of a scientific name is the name of the genus 48

geothermal a renewable energy resource 96

gravitational potential energy energy stored in objects high up 92

gravity the attraction of bodies towards each other as a result of them having mass 116, 122

H

habitats the places where animals and plants live 26

harmful a substance that will damage your body 50

hazards dangers 26, 50, 60, 112

heat energy energy given out by hot objects 92

hemisphere half a sphere; on the Earth, the section above the equator is called the northern hemisphere 126

herbivores animals that eat plants 34

hibernate go into a deep sleep through the winter 30

hormones a group of chemicals secreted in small amounts that control the growth and activities of living things 18, 22

hydro-electric a renewable energy resource 96

hydrochloric acid an acid produced by dissolving hydrogen chloride gas in water 50

hydrogen a flammable gas; it burns to form water 64

I

implantation the settling of an embryo in the lining of the uterus 15

independent variable the variable you decide to change and measure as the input of your experiment 90

indicators substances that change colour to indicate whether a substance is an acid, an alkali or neutral 52

indigestion an uncomfortable feeling in the stomach region as a result of there being too much acid present 58

inherited variations differences that parents pass on to offspring 38

inherit have a feature passed on from a parent 15

insoluble a substance that will not dissolve 88

instinctive inbuilt behaviour of an animal; behaviour that does not have to be learned 30

investigation activity for finding out either information or what happens 30

invertebrates animals without a backbone 44

irritant a substance that will cause itching or slight sores on your body 50

IVF (*in vitro* fertilisation) fertilisation of egg cells in a dish 24

O

observing   investigating an item or what happens using your senses   10, 30

oil   a liquid mixture of many compounds mostly made from hydrogen and carbon found in the Earth's crust; oil was formed from the remains of plants and animals that died millions of years ago; a fossil fuel   94

orbit   the path of a satellite around a planet; the path of a planet around a star   124

organs   structures in a plant or animal made of several different tissues   1, 6

ovary   where egg cells are made   15

oviduct   the tube that carries an egg cell from an ovary to the uterus   15

ovulation   the release of an ovum from an ovary about once a month   15

oxide   compound of oxygen and another element   62

oxygen   a gas in the air   62

P

parallel   an electric circuit in which there are two or more different routes for the electric current   108

partial eclipse   a view of the Moon or Sun in which only part of it is dark, owing to an eclipse   130

particle model of matter   a way of picturing matter as made up of moving particles; also called the kinetic theory   74, 80

particles   very small pieces of matter that everything is made of   74

pH scale   a scale, 0–14, that tells you how acid or alkaline a solution is   54

phases   the different stages in the appearance of the Moon every lunar month   128

placenta   the organ through which a fetus gets food and oxygen and gets rid of waste   19

planets   bodies that orbit a star   128

pollination   transfer of pollen from the anther (male part) to the stigma (female part) of a flower of the same species   12

power supply   pushes the electric current around an electric circuit   104

predators   animals that kill and eat other animals   34

prediction   saying what you think will happen   30

prey   an animal that is eaten by another animal   34

producers   a name given to green plants because they produce food   34

products   new substances made in a chemical reaction   64

puberty   when boys and girls first make sex cells and are able to reproduce   22

pulls   the plural of pull; used to refer to forces in a particular direction; opposite in directionto a push   114

pushes   the plural of push; used to refer to forces in a particular direction; opposite in direction to a pull   114

R

reactants   a substance that you start off with in a chemical reaction   64

reacts   what substances do when they take part in a chemical reaction   56

red blood cells   blood cells that carry oxygen   6

renewable   energy resources that are constantly being replaced and won't get used up   96

reproduction   when living things produce young of the same kind as themselves   10, 15

reptiles   vertebrates with scaly skin and eggs with tough shells   44

T

technical involving the application of a scientific idea or way of working 100

technology the use of scientific ideas or techniques to solve problems 112

technological culture the use of technology in everyday life 122

telescope a device that magnifies objects in the distance 134

testis where sperm (male sex cells) are made in animals; the plural is testes 15

theories ideas to explain evidence 10, 72

thinking distance the distance a car travels between the driver seeing the stop sign and putting on the brakes 120

tides the rising and falling of the sea on the Earth's surface owing to the gravity of the Moon; a possible renewable energy source 96

tilted at an angle to something; the axis that the Earth spins around is tilted compared with the axis of its orbit around the Sun 126

tissues groups of cells with the same shape and job 1, 6

U

umbilical cord contains the blood vessels that carry food, water, oxygen and waste between the placenta and the fetus 20

universal indicator an indicator that has many different colours depending on the pH of the solution that it is in 54

V

vacuole space filled with cell sap in the cytoplasm of a plant cell 4

variables in an experiment, things that can be changed to affect the result 26, 90

variations differences between members of a species 36

vary are different 36

vertebrates animals with a skeleton made of bone inside their body 44

vibrate move backwards and forwards very quickly 74

W

wave a renewable energy resource 96

weak used to describe acids and alkalis that have a pH close to neutral 50

weight the force of gravity on a mass 116

West a direction on the Earth's surface; 90° to left of the line pointing from the South to the North; the opposite direction to East 124

wind a renewable energy resource 96

word equation a way of writing down what happens in a chemical reaction 62

Alamy 7D.HSWb (©Holt Studios International Ltd); **Allsport Concepts / Getty Images** 7G3c (Chris Cole); **Andrew Lambert** 7E.5b; 7F.1e, 7F.1i, 7F.3a, 7F.3b, 7F.3c, 7F.3d; 7J.2a, 7J.HSWa, 7J.HSWe,7J. HSWf; **Art Directors** 7A.2c, 7A.3a, 7A.3g, 7B.2c, 7B.5c, 7C.2a , 7D.1c, 7D.1d, 7D.1e, 7D.5d, 7F.1c, 7F.1f, 7F.1g, 7F.1j, 7F.4a, 7F.4b; **B&C Alexander** 7B.1d; **Biophoto Associates** 7B.4a; **Bruce Coleman Collection** 7C.1a, 7C.1b, 7C.2b, 7C.2c, 7C.2e; **Bubbles Photolibrary** 7B.5a (Jennie Woodcock), 7I.4a (Angela Hampton), 7I.4b (Jennie Woodcock), 7I.4d (Chris Rout); **Corbis** 7A.2b (Bettmann), 7B.HSW (O Franken), 7F.HSWa (Archivo Iconographico S.A.), 7K.HSWa (Sergio Pitaman), 7K.HSWe; **Dave Acaster** 7E.HSW; **Ecoscene** 7I.HSWa (Anthony Cooper); 7I.HSWb (Jim Winkley); **Grant Heilman** 7A.3f (Kent Wood); **Greg Evans Photo Library** 7D.1b, 7D.1f, 7D.1g; **IBM UK Labs** 7J.HSWc; **Ida Cook** 7F.1a, 7F.1b; **The Image Bank / Getty Images** 7G.3b (Patti McConville); **Janice Weidel** 7D.1a; **John Adds** 7A.3c; **Mary Evans Photo Library** 7D.2a, 7D.2b, 7D.2c; **Microscopix** 7A.2a (Andrew Syred); **National Maritime Museum, London** 7K.HSWb; **Natural History Museum, London** 7D.HSWa; **naturepl.com** 7C.HSW (Kim Taylor); **NASA** 7L.5a; **NHPA** 7C.1c (Micheal Tweedie), 7C.2d (Stephen Dalton), 7I.2a (Daniel Huedin); **Olivia Johnston** 7E.4a; **Oxford Scientific Films** 7B.1c (Michael Fogden), 7D.5b (Mark Hamblin), 7D.5c (Konrad Wothe), 7D.5e (David Tipling), 7D.5f (OSF), 7D.5g (OSF), 7D.5h (London Scientific Films); **Philip Harris Education** 7K.1a; **Science Photo Library** 7A.1a (Alfred Pasieka), 7A.3b (Dr Gopal Murti), 7A.3d (Astrid & Hans-Freide Michler), 7A.3e (Claud Nurilsang & Marc Perenou), 7B.1a (D Philips), 7B.1b (CNRI), 7B.2a (CC Studios), 7B.2b (Gary Parker), 7B.5b (Mark Clarke), 7B.5d (Mark Clarke), 7D.1h (Peter Menzel), 7D.4a (Prof P Motta), 7D.5a (David Aubrey), 7E.5a (Prof. P. Motta), 7F.1d (Martin Bond), 7F.1h (Jerry Mason), 7F.HSWb Andrew McCleanaghan 7G.2a (Northwestern Univesity Library), 7G.3a (Martin Dohrn), 7G.HSWa, 7G.HSWb (US Library of Congress), 7I.1a (David Duscros), 7I.1b (Jim Selby), 7I.1c (Alan & Sandy Carey), 7I.1d (Simon Fraser), 7I.1e (Deep Light Productions), 7I.1f (David Nunak), 7I.1g (Alan Sirulnikoff), 7I.1h (Martin Bond), 7I.2b (Mark Clarke), 7I.4c (Simon Fraser), 7I.4e (David Frazier/Agstock), 7J.HSWb (Maximilian Stock Ltd), 7J.HSWd (Sheila Terry), 7K.HSWd (John Howard), 7K.HSWb (US Library of Congress), 7L.3a (Pekka Parviainen), 7L.3b (John Sandford), 7L.4a (Dr Fred Espenak), 7L.4b (Dr Fred Espenak), 7L.5b (NASA), 7L.5c (NASA), 7L.5d (NASA), 7L.HSW(Matthew Oldfield); **Still Pictures** 7E.5c (Mark Edwards); **The Dean and Chapter of York** 7F.3e, 7F.3f; **Vanessa Miles** 7H.2a, 7K.4a; **Wellcome Library London** 7A.2d, 7E.1a, 7A.HSW

Image references show the Unit and Topic of the book (eg. 7A.1) and the order of the image in the Topic from top to bottom, left to right (e.g. 7A.1b is the second photograph in Topic 1 of Unit 7A).

Series advisors Andy Cooke, Jean Martin
Series authors Sam Ellis, Jean Martin

Series consultants Diane Fellowes-Freeman, Richard Needham

Based on original material by Derek Baron, Trevor Bavage, Paul Butler, Andy Cooke, Zoe Crompton, Sam Ellis, Kevin Frobisher, Jean Martin, Mick Mulligan, Chris Ram